W9-AEP-753

A Perfect Word
for
Every Occasion

A PERFECT WORD

for

EVERY OCCASION

LIZ DUCKWORTH

BETHANY HOUSE PUBLISHERS
a division of Baker Publishing Group
Minneapolis, Minnesota

© 2012 by Bethany House Publishers

Published by Bethany House Publishers
11400 Hampshire Avenue South
Bloomington, Minnesota 55438
www.bethanyhouse.com

Bethany House Publishers is a division of
Baker Publishing Group, Grand Rapids, Michigan

Printed in the United States of America

All rights reserved. No part of this publication may be reproduced, stored in a retrieval system, or transmitted in any form or by any means—for example, electronic, photocopy, recording—without the prior written permission of the publisher. The only exception is brief quotations in printed reviews.

Library of Congress Cataloging-in-Publication Data
Duckworth, Liz.
    A perfect word for every occasion : ideal for letters, receiving lines, Facebook, emails, thank-you notes, condolences—and much more / Liz Duckworth.
        p.   cm.
    Includes bibliographical references.
    Summary: "Things to say, lines to write, and Scripture verses to share on any occasion (when someone is sick or grieving, on birthdays, for weddings and engagements, in thank you notes, etc.) and in any way (Facebook messages, emails, cards, receiving lines, texting, and more)"—Provided by publisher.
    ISBN 978-0-7642-1022-8 (pbk. : alk. paper)
    1. Interpersonal communication—Religious aspects—Christianity. 2. Oral communication—Religious aspects—Christianity. 3. Written communication—Religious aspects—Christianity. I. Title.
BV4597.53.C64D83 2012
395.4—dc23   2012013963

Scripture quotations are from the Holy Bible, New International Version®. NIV®. Copyright © 1973, 1978, 1984, 2011 by Biblica, Inc.™ Used by permission of Zondervan. All rights reserved worldwide. www.zondervan.com

The Internet addresses, email addresses, and phone numbers in this book are accurate at the time of publication. They are provided as a resource. Baker Publishing Group does not endorse them or vouch for their content or permanence.

Cover design by Dan Pitts

12   13   14   15   16   17   18   7   6   5   4   3   2   1

R0427473155

Contents

Introduction

That day at work was a hard one for Rob. It was his first day back in two weeks—two weeks missed because his daughter was born with a rare disorder and lived only a week. What was supposed to be a joyful time ended with crushed dreams and a baby's funeral.

Rob knew his co-workers at the Christian publishing company had been praying for him and his family. Of course they cared. And that's why he was mystified that by the end of his first day back, not one person said anything to him about his loss. Not a mention. Not a word.

It left him feeling lonely and lost.

Most of us have found ourselves on the other side of this story. We know someone has been through pain and loss, but we find ourselves in a frozen place. A place where we want to offer help, but we're too afraid of saying the wrong thing to say anything at all. We are at a loss for words. We buy a sympathy card, which doesn't seem to express what we really feel, and sign it. Without the right words, we end up sad but feeling helpless.

Our loss for words isn't always such a heavy matter. It's not that we don't care, but we're in a huge hurry. Our plates are full. Life is flying by at top speed and we are barely able to think, let alone send meaningful messages. Life's major occasions come at us from every direction, and our ability to mark them well slips through our fingers.

Or we're lost for words because we wonder what's left to say that's new under the sun. Where I work, we pass around birthday cards for everybody to sign. When it's time to jot my special thoughts into a two-inch square of space, my brain blanks out. That's better than Jeff, though. He was on autopilot one day when he scribbled Happy Birthday in bold letters with three exclamation points—onto the sympathy card for Bill, who lost his father. There's still a use for Wite-Out in this high-tech world of ours.

What happened? Why do we often find ourselves at a complete loss for words, or looking for the right words in all the wrong places?

When looking to place blame, I'd like to thank the Internet. Our computers, iPads, and smartphones are portals to a million trillion billion words. So many words on the World Wide Web: gigs and bytes and an infinity of information. More words than people have ever before had at their fingertips. So thank you, Internet, for giving us so many words, yet often leaving us speechless.

Is it just me? Because I think somehow the act of pushing a button to instantly find anything has robbed us of the ability to access our own heart to find the right words at the right time.

Words of comfort and care.

Words of sympathy and understanding.

Words of truth and joy.

Words that say exactly what we feel.

Okay. It's not just technology's fault. It's our culture, our fast-paced lives, our lack of practice crafting what we write.

Sure, our words are dashed off in an email, tweeted on Twitter, or posted as the latest Facebook status. Words: We've got a million of 'em, and they are flying through cyberspace at breakneck speed.

It's not that we don't have enough words. We have so many words, we don't know where to even begin when it's time to:

- write the perfect message on a card we hope will be saved and savored by someone we love;
- find the right words to comfort another in the wake of grief and loss;
- join a friend, colleague, or relative at any point in life's journey—a birth, graduation, or retirement—and share understanding.

I believe in the power of our God-given hearts and minds to tap in to the creativity and thought needed to reach out to people around us. And as believers, we have the Spirit to guide us toward grace-filled words. What we lack is practice.

Back in the olden days of yore, people had a lot more practice with notes, cards, and correspondence. Long-distance phone calls were expensive, so that left the mail to deliver insights into daily life. As a young married woman, I was excited to receive a plain postcard from my grandma every few weeks. She'd type on it front and back, leaving a tiny space for my address. She included tidbits about her world: *The hail wiped out the corn. Grandpa put out a prairie fire just in time. Bridge club is coming over for cards.* Her little notes were poetry of precision and love typed out single-spaced. You don't see that much anymore.

At Compassion International, where I work, a big part of our child sponsorship ministry enables sponsors to write encouraging letters to children in poverty. Many struggle with letter writing because it's a foreign activity these days. These good people want to reach out to sponsored kids but don't know what to say or how to say it. Of course, it's often a new experience for our sponsored kids too. Daniel, my fourteen-year-old sponsored teen from Ecuador, recently wrote and asked if there were condors in Chicago. (Maybe I confused him by sending photos from a Chicago business trip. Sadly, I never saw a condor there.) It's so hard to cross the bridge between lives, cultures, and backgrounds with only a few precious words.

Still, we can get back what we've lost to the intensity of our Internet age. And in discovering how to find our best words, we can learn to know ourselves and grow closer to people in our lives. It's a lesson in empathy. A curriculum of caring.

To help you, this book is filled with ideas, shortcuts, exercises, and examples.

It's not a substitute for searching for words. It just offers signposts along the way in your own journey.

Okay, sometimes it will get you where you're going a little faster. Help you write that card or make that memorable statement. But I hope it will give you much more than a template for your thoughts.

I hope these words will guide you in our rush-rush world to a slower pace. May you find a place where you can tap your real feelings and express them with honesty and wisdom.

With wit and encouragement. Saying what you want to say, the way you wish to say it.

I've included lots of Scripture passages too. God's Word is filled with truth we can share at special times. My efforts may save you the need to flip pages, Google sporadically, or dust off your ancient concordance. (For those of you who've never heard of a concordance, it's like BibleGateway.com in hard copy.)

Finally, to further ease your journey toward grace-filled words, I'm including some "what not to say" examples. Think of them as do-not-enter or bridge-out-ahead signs, keeping you from making a wrong turn. Though I believe it's better to say or write the wrong thing than to offer nothing at all, it's even better to avoid a misstep if you can.

God's Word tells us that a word fitly spoken is "like apples of gold in settings of silver" (Proverbs 25:11). Imagine an apple of gold—especially at today's gold prices. The incredible value. The shine, the beauty. The lack of actual nutrients. (Scratch that. My metaphor has broken down.) Who wouldn't love to find a golden apple?

I trust your own words "fitly spoken" will fill the lives of those you care about with amazing joy, comfort, and more riches than an apple of gold. Or a whole bushel of them!

> Let your conversation be always full of grace, seasoned with salt, so that you may know how to answer everyone.
>
> Colossians 4:6

1

Words for the Grieving

Let's jump into the deep end and tackle the toughest topic first. Writing letters and notes to people who have suffered a painful loss can be a very sensitive and difficult task.

It's such a hard task that we might react by postponing it, starting then stopping, or distracting ourselves until we can get into the right state of mind. That's a description of me "not-writing" this chapter. I frittered and fought myself. Picked up a pen. Put it down. Took walks, read Facebook and Twitter, and finally broke down and dusted the house. Anything to face thinking about what it takes to offer comfort through written words.

Why is it so tough? Because consoling people in grief requires us to follow a dark road leading to a place we don't want to be. In order to reach out to people who are hurting in the deepest way, we have to hurt too. And we are forced to think about subjects we'd rather avoid: death, loss, heartbreak, and pain.

Writing even a short note on a sympathy card requires us to walk with a person in grief and empathize with his or her feelings. It's not easy and it's not pleasant, yet it is a vital act of community and connection. Offering a message of heartfelt condolence is a ministry all by itself. It's an act of service and sacrifice that asks us to put others before ourselves as we travel—if even for only a few steps—along their journey of loss.

In acknowledging the difficulty of writing words of true sympathy, imagine the personal sacrifice of this man: Secretary of Defense Robert Gates. After five years of service, he was preparing to step down in June of 2011. The job was taking a major emotional toll on him, because he had been writing a personal note to the family of every soldier who died under his command. His emotions were evident in his interview with Diane Sawyer of ABC News, as he said, "I swore when I took the job I would never allow any of these kids to become a statistic for me.

"I go to the hospitals, I go to Arlington. I see their families, so I feel the human cost. And that's why I told somebody the other day, maybe it is time for me to leave, because these things have begun to weigh on me in a way that maybe I'm not as useful as I used to be," Secretary Gates said.[1]

It was time for Gates to make a change and put aside the burden of comforting others on such a vast scale. But his compassion for suffering families provides a tremendous example of the importance of reaching out to the grieving, regardless of personal cost.

Sometimes the most difficult part of sharing with one who has suffered a loss involves knowing how to begin. So read the following ideas and guidelines, and consider the prompts created to help you get started. In each chapter of this book, you'll first be guided to find your own words, then you'll see a list of examples to adapt to your own style and situation. You'll also find some helpful Scripture passages as well as examples of what *not* to say.

Guidelines for Finding the Right Words

While handwriting is becoming rarer these days, nothing says "personal" or "thoughtful" like a handwritten message on a card or in a note. Sending an email or posting a Facebook message might be easier or more convenient for you, of course—and there's no reason you can't quickly reach out to acknowledge a loss through these ephemeral forms—but by taking the time to work through your personal expression in the form of a handwritten note or letter, you will better communicate how much you care and offer real comfort.

It's a good idea to keep a scratch pad—an inexpensive notebook where you can scribble down your first thoughts, scratch out your false starts, and write rough drafts of your letters, notes, or even those few personal lines added to a thoughtfully chosen card. This helps you avoid the pressure of facing that blank space on a card, and helps you formulate the right words the first time around.

Identify words that describe how you feel. They don't have to be fancy; use simple words such as *sad, sorry, lost, hurt,* or *heartbroken.* These plain but honest words can apply to your own personal response to the loss, as well as describe how you feel for the person to whom you are communicating.

God's Word directs us to "rejoice with those who rejoice; mourn with those who mourn" (Romans 12:15). We are to come alongside in happiness as well as in difficult times. Remember that sharing with others in their times of loss is a God-honoring activity that promises comfort and the building up of the Body of Christ. It is a means of truly building up one another.

As believers, we have the privilege of a relationship with Jesus Christ. We can share the joy of hope with those in the Body of Christ and remind each other of God's wonderful promises. Yet it's important to be sure that we are sharing truth. If you are not certain about someone's relationship with the Lord, avoid making assumptions either way. Focus on the relationship, the event, the feelings that are part of this loss.

A helpful example in the Bible comes from John 11:1–44, the account of Jesus raising Lazarus from the dead. When Jesus learned His good friend Lazarus had died, He went to Bethany and encountered Lazarus's distraught sisters, Mary and Martha. The John 11:35 passage is simple in its powerful description: "Jesus wept." The Son of God expressed His very human feelings through tears of compassion, identifying with the pain the sisters were experiencing and weeping along with them.

Remember that shared pain is often easier to carry.

Prompts to Help You Begin

These are aids that can help you clarify your thoughts and get started. Choose one or two activities to prompt you as you prepare to write.

- What does the person you are writing to mean to you? What role does he or she play in your life? How can you affirm this person and your relationship? For example, "As my boss, you are such a role model to me"; "As my aunt, you have always been there for me"; "As a friend, you are such an important part of my life." This affirmation may or may not find its way into your note, but it will help you center your thoughts as you write.

- Think about the one who has died. What were some outstanding qualities he or she brought to life? What impact did this person have on the people in his or her world? How did this person meaningfully affect you? Think of a specific example.

- What wishes do you have for the person to whom you are writing? Jot down a few words that may complete one or more of the following statements.

    I hope . . .

    May the Lord . . .

    May those around you . . .

    Please know that . . .

- Read the Scripture passages that follow later in this chapter and pray before you start writing. Let your heart and mind be inspired by the Lord, and ask Him to lead you to create a message of comfort and encouragement.

Words to Make Your Own

These examples may serve to inspire you or can be adapted into your own words.

In order to make them general, I mostly used generic descriptions (such as "your beautiful daughter"). Of course, naming the person and being as specific as possible about the individual who passed away is a great comfort to those left behind to mourn that person's death.

Remembering the one who is gone is so important that you may want to send another note months or even a year later, just to let the grieving one know that their loved one lives on in memory.

For the Loss of a Spouse

- He was such a caring husband and father. May God surround you with His loving arms as you grieve the loss of your beloved companion in this life.
- I smile when I think of your dear wife and all she gave to all of our lives. She brought joy to so many in her world!
- I pray you'll find support from family and friends and hope for the future, and that you'll experience God's presence in a very real way during this very difficult time.
- As you walk down this dark path, please know you are not alone. You remain in my thoughts and prayers, and those of many others during this time of sadness and pain.
- Memories of [your wife/husband] come flooding back at this time, reminding me of what a loving, giving person she/he was. It's hard to imagine what you are going through right now, but I hope you remember how many people love you and want to be there for you.
- How I want to reach across the miles and hug you right now. I am praying for you and trusting God for His comfort in your loss.
- I wish I could take away the pain you are going through. May God grant you the comfort of friends and family and wonderful memories that can never be lost.

For the Loss of a Child

- Words fail to express how deeply sorry I am to learn of the terrible loss of your precious child.
- May the God of all comfort make a way through this sorrow for you.
- We remember so many happy times with your beautiful daughter, and we hurt deeply for you and all the family in this time of pain and loss.
- There is no way to begin to share our heartbreak over the loss of your beloved son.

For the Loss of a Parent, a Close Family Member, or Shared Family Member

- I am so sorry for your loss. I will miss him.
- It's always hard to lose a loved one, and we wanted to let you know our thoughts are with you.
- I am praying that you will find comfort in God's unchanging Word and His steadfast love.
- We pray that during these difficult days you will know the comfort of the Lord as you grieve and, ultimately, find comfort in His healing.
- It must have meant so much for you to be there. Someone to share sorrow is often the only real comfort we feel when we lose someone so precious.
- You have been so much on my mind since I learned of this sad loss. I grieve for and with each of you. The family is so important to me, and I'm grateful for the love and support it offers.
- We know you and your family are grieving, and we ask the Lord to help you at this sad time.

For the Loss of a Parent When Death Was Not Unexpected

- I have just learned of your mother's death. I know that even when expected, it makes for a sad and difficult time. Please know that you are very much in my prayers and heart.
- It is always hard to lose a parent, and we wanted to let you know our thoughts and prayers are with you.
- I know you felt the space your dad left right away. Even though our parents are in declining health, it's still a shock when we lose them.
- We are thinking of you and praying for you in the loss of your mother. It is a time of mixed emotions. The Lord keeps His word—that we can count on.
- These past years and especially recent months must have been so hard for you. Keep the happy memories and let the others fade.

For the Loss of a Friend

- May you find hope in the promises of God and the love of friends who care.
- My heart goes out to you as you grieve the loss of your friend.
- In this sad time, please know that I hurt with you and for you.
- May God grant the comfort that only He can during these difficult days.
- I share such a warm memory of your friend. What a tragic loss, one I pray God will ease with time.

For the Loss of a Colleague

- I know you will miss your co-worker and friend a great deal. May God be very close to you in this time of loss and transition.
- In tough times like this, it's good to know others are praying. You are in my thoughts and prayers regularly.
- Your loss of your colleague is such a difficult one. Please know that I care.

For the Loss of a Pet

- I often saw what an important part of your life your pet was. May you find comfort in the happy memories of time spent together.
- Losing a pet is such a sad and painful experience. Please know that I care.
- (Describe a specific memory of the pet who died. Here's an example.) Remember when we took that hike with your dog through the autumn leaves last fall? I'm so glad to have such a happy memory to share, even during this hard time as you grieve the loss of your beloved pet.
- (If you have a photo that includes the pet and its owner, share a copy along with your note.) I hope this photo brings a smile during these tough days after the loss of your cat. I know how much she brought to your life.
- As you grieve the loss of your much-loved pet, may you be comforted by your friends.
- (Since pets don't have funerals, think of a way to offer a time of remembering and closure. Here's an example.)

Please let me know if you want to go out for coffee. We can share happy memories of times with [name of pet], if that will help you work through this sad loss.

Talking Points: What to Say in a Receiving Line

Whether you are going through a receiving line at a funeral, or speaking with a bereaved person at a visitation, keep a few points in mind to avoid a last-minute stumble. The deep feelings we experience at these moments can sometimes cause us to freeze up or draw a blank. Just remember that it's not about you, and your words aren't nearly as important as your heartfelt sympathy.

Avoid these clichés, which can be misinterpreted or may unintentionally sound more thoughtless than comforting:

- I know exactly how you feel.
- It's God's will; it was just her time.
- Keep your chin up.
- At least he didn't suffer.
- You must feel relieved that it's over.

Keep your words simple and sincere. You don't have to be original; just be real. Some appropriate comments include:

- I am truly sorry for your loss.
- My condolences to you and your family.
- [Name of deceased] will be deeply missed.
- [Name of deceased] was an amazing person.
- It was a pleasure knowing him/her.
- I am praying for you and the whole family.

If you are attending a funeral and aren't well-known to those in the receiving line, be sure to explain how you know the deceased. You may want to briefly share a positive memory as well.

Aunt Me-me's Guide to What *Not* to Say

Meet Aunt Me-me. Sure, she's fictional, but she's also sweet, outgoing, generous, and spontaneous. Maybe a little too spontaneous. She serves a useful purpose in this book by illustrating the wrong turns we all want to avoid while reaching out to others. Without intending to, any of us can be Aunt Me-me at one time or another. In wanting to help, we unintentionally give the wrong message, one of insensitivity or uncaring.

It's not that Aunt Me-me doesn't care about other people. She has many friends and relatives, and she's actively involved in their lives. But when it comes to finding the right words for specific losses or other life passages, dear Me-me stumbles. Why? Because in the midst of powerful emotions and overwhelming feelings, sweet Aunt Me-me defaults to *her* emotions and *her* feelings. It's all about *me* for Me-me.

Though she wants to give comfort, the pain she personally feels causes her great anxiety. This leads to awkward attempts to cheer people up in order to get past her own discomfort. She puts too much emphasis on her *own* responses, reactions, and history. So she winds up being insensitive. Instead of comforting, she ends up sending mixed messages.

Aunt Me-me often minimizes other people's feelings. Instead of getting in touch with her real thoughts, she leans on clichés and superficial assurances. Worse, she offers pat answers instead of coming alongside with her true, heartfelt words.

These are a few of Me-me's well-meant mistakes, made in her rush to respond at a time of loss:

- It's for the best.
- He's in a better place.
- God won't give you more than you can handle.
- Time heals all wounds.
- I'll never get over this terrible loss.
- (In the case of miscarriage) Don't stop trying. You'll have another baby. I know God wants you to be a parent.
- The Bible says, "All things work together for good." It will all work out.

As illustrated above, too often Me-me is trying to ease her own pain, to get past the intense work of grief and return to an easier place.

Unfortunately, there are no easy paths through loss. Grief requires us to hurt and to be honest about the pain, not to lessen it or rush through it. Honest words that come from the heart reflect that reality and require us to take time with the process.

What Others Say: Quotes Worth Sharing

God gave us our memories so that we might have roses in December.

James M. Barrie

Friendships multiply joys and divide griefs.

H. G. Bohn

Hope is faith holding out its hand in the dark.

George Iles

Recall it as often as you wish, a happy memory never wears out.

Libbie Fudim

There is no fence or hedge round time that has gone. You can go back and have what you like if you remember it well enough.

Richard Llewellyn, *How Green Was My Valley*

What lies behind us and what lies before us are tiny matters compared to what lies within us.

Ralph Waldo Emerson

Only love can be divided endlessly and still not diminish.

Anne Morrow Lindbergh

Love is a fruit in season at all times, and within reach of every hand.

Mother Teresa of Calcutta

May every sunrise hold more promise, every moonrise hold more peace.

Anonymous

Scripture Passages to Read or Quote

"Though the mountains be shaken
and the hills be removed,
yet my unfailing love for you will not be shaken
nor my covenant of peace be removed,"
says the LORD, who has compassion on you.

Isaiah 54:10

Yet this I call to mind
and therefore I have hope:
Because of the LORD's great love we are not
consumed,
for his compassions never fail.
They are new every morning;
great is your faithfulness.
I say to myself, "The LORD is my portion;
therefore I will wait for him."

Lamentations 3:21–24

There is a time for everything,
and a season for every activity under the heavens:
a time to be born and a time to die,
a time to plant and a time to uproot,
a time to kill and a time to heal,
a time to tear down and a time to build,
a time to weep and a time to laugh,
a time to mourn and a time to dance. . . .
He has made everything beautiful in its time.

Ecclesiastes 3:1–4, 11

Where, O death, is your victory?
Where, O death, is your sting?

1 Corinthians 15:55

The LORD is close to the brokenhearted
and saves those who are crushed in spirit.

Psalm 34:18

No, in all these things we are more than conquerors through
him who loved us. For I am convinced that neither death nor
life, neither angels nor demons, neither the present nor the

future, nor any powers, neither height nor depth, nor anything else in all creation, will be able to separate us from the love of God that is in Christ Jesus our Lord.

Romans 8:37–39

Even though I walk through the darkest valley, I will fear no evil, for you are with me; your rod and your staff, they comfort me.

Psalm 23:4

May your unfailing love be my comfort, according to your promise to your servant.

Psalm 119:76

Then young women will dance and be glad, young men and old as well. I will turn their mourning into gladness; I will give them comfort and joy instead of sorrow.

Jeremiah 31:13

The God and Father of our Lord Jesus Christ [is] the Father of compassion and the God of all comfort.

2 Corinthians 1:3

2

Words of Gratitude

Gratitude is an attitude almost everybody agrees is key to a happy and balanced life. On the other hand, expressing gratitude in the form of thank-you notes is sometimes a loaded subject. There are lots of funny stories and jokes that take a poke at getting kids to actually write words of thanks, or tattling on those who don't know how to say thank-you properly.

One old joke describes a mom who decides one Christmas that she's tired of nagging her kids about the need to write thank-you notes. As a result, that year Grandpa never gets any thank-you's for the very generous checks he's written to the kids.

The following year, however, things turn out differently. "All the kids came over personally to thank me," Grandpa tells his friend with a chuckle.

"That's great," says his friend. "Why did they change their ways this year?"

"That's easy," declares Grandpa. "This year I didn't sign the checks."

Ingratitude isn't always the reason that a handwritten thank-you note doesn't turn up in the mailbox. I know of one young married woman with an embarrassing story: "We had about 150 guests attend our wedding two years ago. I spent weeks preparing the thank-you notes. I gave a stack of them to my husband to get addresses from my mother-in-law. I guess I just assumed that he mailed them afterward. Well, to my horror, a few weeks ago, I found these notes in the bottom of a box that I was unpacking. I felt absolutely horrible; his family must think I'm so ungrateful."

She planned to type up a note explaining that she found the un-mailed notes, and that she was embarrassed that they were never sent out. And for proof, she would include in the envelopes the original thank-you notes. She promised not to blame her husband. We'll see how well that works out!

My nephew and his wife are very busy parents of two adorable daughters. Though they live far away, they post a lot on Facebook, which helps me keep up with family adventures and the girls' growing-up. All this e-news is great, but I appreciate their approach to a recent thank-you note. It seems many months (okay, more than a year) had slipped by since their youngest was born. But they took time to send a very creative thank-you recently, accompanied by a whole page of family photos. I was so tickled to read the note, "written" (with help) by little Jewelianna:

Dear Aunt Beth and family,
Thank you so much for the gifts you sent me. I'm sorry this is so late, but my mom has been trying to get

*accustomed to handling 2 kids and looking for time
to write the family. She still isn't used to it yet! Maybe
after Evelyn and I turn 18. . . . Hope everyone is well!
We are all doing great. (I'm walking and "talking" now!)*

Love,
Jewelianna

As a once-young mother of two, I know how tough it is to
get out those handwritten thank-you notes, and I just smiled
to receive this one because it was filled with such love and
creativity.

Guidelines for Finding the Right Words

The basic thank-you note has three simple elements. A key
aspect is tying the gift to the giver, and keeping it as specific
and personal as possible. Remember, a verbal thank-you really
is no substitute for a note. Neither is e-thanks via email or
social networking.

So when you pick up your pen, keep these three steps in mind:

- Focus on the giver, expressing something about your
  relationship and what the gift-giver means to you.
- Recognize the specific gift and explain why it's special
  to you.
- Extend a hope or wish about the future of this gift and
  the giver in your life.

Here's a great example of a thoughtful thank-you from
a note sent by my good friend Michelle. For her birthday I
sent earrings shaped like the infinity symbol because we had

been talking about the importance of living lives that focus on God's infinite love and abundance. She wrote:

Thank you so much for the amazing earrings. I love the meaning you put behind them—infinite abundance. Love it! I wear them daily, to keep reminding me. I look forward to catching up with you. So much to tell you this Sunday (though I'm sure you'll get this after our call). I am so blessed to have you in my life. God bless!

Michelle's note is simple but truly heartfelt and filled with her own enthusiasm and personal expression. Some words are underlined, and there are arrows and exclamation points. Her personality comes through in her handwriting, and that's partly why I love getting notes like this. They capture relationships in multiple ways and affirm how important we are to each other.

In addition to receiving material gifts or cash gifts, sometimes we write to thank someone for their gift of friendship or a thoughtful act. These notes can be more challenging because we need to identify what the gift really is and how much it has affected our world. Just as these kind acts are powerful, the expression of thanks is equally powerful.

I remember how it brought tears to my eyes to read the following letter in my local paper:

We would like to thank the gentleman who anonymously paid for our 60th anniversary dinner at the Olive Garden on July 28. We have no idea of his identity, as he was at a table behind us and overheard our conversation with the waitress about our anniversary. When he left, he paid for our meal including dessert. The waitress then told us what he had done.

All one reads or hears on the news is about the bad that happens in the world, and we wanted to pass on some good news that happened to us. There are good and kind people in our world, also. We wanted all to know that there are fine people out there and it was our pleasure to have been the recipients of his kindness.

Thank you, sir, whoever you are. And may God bless you.[2]

A well-written thank-you is a testimony to goodness bestowed on you. Giving thanks is woven through God's Word: "Give thanks in all circumstances; for this is God's will for you in Christ Jesus" (1 Thessalonians 5:18). A heart of thanksgiving is a sign of one who walks with the Lord and knows the true source of all our gifts and blessings.

Still, while the Bible is filled with examples of thankfulness in action, it really lacks examples of nicely phrased thank-you notes. For some reason I couldn't help imagining favorite biblical greats writing as if they were acquainted with contemporary etiquette.

Dear Delilah,
 Thank you so much for this delightful new haircut. Your flair for fashion is amazing! While it's a lot shorter than I usually wear it, it really is cool for summer, like you promised. Sorry to cut this short, but somebody's pounding on the door.

    Love and hugs,
    Samson

Dear Eve,
 I want you to know how much I appreciate your recent gift of an apple. Though I couldn't help noticing

it already had a bite taken out of it, I was moved by your willingness to share. Now, do you think you could spare some of those fig leaves that look so becoming on you? Actually, one should do it. You're the best!

Your man,
Adam

Dear Dad,
    Wow, you really outdid yourself with the coat. I love the many colors! It fits perfectly and makes me feel like a king. I know nothing bad can happen to me when I'm dressed in such a great coat. (Just don't tell my bros how much you spent on it, okay?)

Your favorite son,
Joe

Prompts to Help You Begin

As you start to write, spend a few minutes thinking about the gift or act of kindness you received. Answer some of these questions in your scratch pad:

- Who gave me the gift?
- What are my favorite qualities about this person?
- Why do I need this gift?
- How will I use it?
- How do I feel about receiving this gift? (Happy? Excited? Appreciated? Valued? Loved?)
- What do I wish for the person who gave me this gift?

Recall a memory connected to the person who gave you the gift. Does it tie in to the gift in any way? Is it part of a shared interest or experience? That memory may prompt something personal and meaningful to include in your note.

What have you learned from the person who gave you this gift? Jot down some ideas in your notebook and search them for something appropriate to include in your message.

Read through the Scripture passages at the end of this chapter and ask God to help you experience a true heart of thankfulness. You may want to include a quote from God's Word in your thank-you note, or simply be inspired by real examples of thanksgiving.

Words to Make Your Own

Remember, these examples are designed to inspire your own words and ideas. I hope they provide you with a wider variety of ideas beyond the standard "thank-you" template.

For a Gift of Money

- Thank you, dear Uncle Bill, for your generous birthday gift. As a poor college student, I can make good use of it for a rare splurge. I'm planning to use it to see a film in an actual movie theater. With popcorn!
- I can't thank you enough, Grandma, for contributing to my college fund. Your faith in me encourages me to keep studying and working toward graduation day.
- Your generous gift came at just the right time. Thank you so much for helping us start our married lives with all those "little things" that we'll be using for years to come.

- It was so thoughtful for you to send a Christmas letter along with a check for the family. We plan to use it for some new board games that will keep us laughing on family nights. We look forward to your visit next year so you can join in!

For a Material Gift

- The clothes you sent for Bobby are so adorable! We loved the baseball theme, as you surely knew we would. Thanks for all the great memories of games watched and shared. We'll think of you when we dress up our little guy in some of his very first "uniforms"!
- Thank you so much for the thoughtful graduation gift. How did you know that was just what I needed? I'll always remember this special occasion, and you, when I use it.
- I was so excited to open the wrapping paper and find the perfect gift! You know me so well. Thank you for spending time and going to the trouble of mailing me the perfect birthday gift. You are a wonderful and caring friend.
- We were touched to receive the lovely frame and photo as an anniversary gift. As we grow older, we continually appreciate special friends like you who share our lives and our memories. Thank you so much for your thoughtfulness and for all you mean to us.

For Friendship

- There's no special occasion, just a very special friendship to celebrate. Thank you for the gift of your presence in my life.

- I'm so glad you are my friend. We have been through ups and downs, good times and hard times. Yet it's always been easier because you are by my side, ready to help or celebrate.

- Thanks for making my life better. God has blessed me with your friendship.

- Who has been there for me when I moved? When I was sick? When I needed to talk? You, that's who. Thanks for always being there.

- You are the definition of friendship. I look forward to many more years of fun and laughs together.

- You are a true example of one who follows Jesus. Thank you for being a godly friend, one with integrity and honesty. Friends like you are rare.

For a Gift of Thoughtfulness

- It really has been tough around here, but we did smile when you dropped off such a delicious meal. Please know how much your care and concern has meant to all of us.

- Well, I know you've been down that road of a growing family! So your gift of baby-sitting the kids for the entire weekend meant all the more to us. We can't thank you enough for sharing your time and caring for the kids so we could have a much-needed break. May God bless you!

- It was so thoughtful of you to invite me out for coffee and a talk in the middle of this difficult time. Thank you for reaching out and helping me in such a concrete way.

- What a joy it was to receive the flowers you sent in memory of Mom. She would have loved the bright colors, and each time we saw them, we remembered that you are praying for us in this time of loss. Thank you with all our hearts.

For Kind Words

- "As iron sharpens iron, so one person sharpens another" (Proverbs 27:17). Thanks for taking time to talk with me and help me think through my future. Your ideas are always helpful and greatly appreciated.
- Just when I needed encouragement, you came along and lifted me up. Thank you for seeing what I needed and meeting that need today. You are a gift from God!
- These aren't easy days, but you have eased some of the pain with your helpful presence and kind words.
- May God bless you for sharing with me today. It helps to learn from your experiences and know you care so much.
- "The quiet words of the wise are more to be heeded than the shouts of a ruler of fools" (Ecclesiastes 9:17). You can't know how much I needed to hear your wise words. Thank you so much for your kindness and insight.

Aunt Me-me's Guide to What *Not* to Say

Before we get to Aunt Me-me's mistakes, here's a story I heard about one couple's wrongheaded approach to wedding thank-you's. Fortunately, the recipient seems to be a model of grace in this case study, shared by Mary (names changed to protect the guilty).

I recently visited my dad, and I happened to notice an interesting postcard in his workshop. When I pointed it out, he shook his head, laughed, and held it out to me. It turned out to be a thank-you card for a wedding gift. On one side was a picture of the happy couple in wedding clothes, while the other side had a printed message that read something like this:

Thank you for being there for Harry and Sally's special day. It meant a lot to us. Thank you for the _____.

Harry and Sally

Handwritten in the blank space was the word *money*. The couple didn't even sign the card! I guess they printed out a bunch of these, identified a gift for each one, and just mailed them out. I was pretty surprised, but my dad said that they were young and probably didn't know better. And at least they sent a card . . . a card worth keeping.

Okay, even clueless Aunt Me-me wouldn't go that far. But she might be tempted to save time and effort by using a sort of template for her thank-you's. You can imagine it: Dear (blank), Thank you so much for the (blank). It was just what I needed. You are so thoughtful. Again, thank you very much. Sincerely, Me-me.

This format will save time, but it's pretty obvious to the recipient that little effort went into a bland note like that. A few more minutes and care will yield a truly meaningful message that will be treasured for a very long time.

Here are some other no-no's from Me-me:

- I'm sorry it took so long to send you this note, but I've been very busy with important matters. (It should go without saying that putting off your thank-you notes is never the best idea. What does procrastination communicate? That thanking the giver just isn't all that important.)

- The sweater you sent was the wrong size. Fortunately I was able to have it tailored into a darling jacket for Fifi. (It might be difficult to know what to say when a gift is the wrong size or color. Think hard about how to graciously acknowledge the present, while being honest about the outcome. If a gift receipt was included and you exchanged the gift for something more appropriate, explain the situation as positively and with as many thank-you's as possible!)

- Thank you so much for the puce tablecloth. I really don't deserve it!

- Thanks for sending $20 for my birthday. I'll include it in my facelift fund. Only $9,980 more to go! (It's considered bad form to name the amount of a cash gift. Just write something like "thank you for remembering me with a thoughtful check" or "I greatly appreciate your generous gift." It's a great idea to mention what you will do with the money, though.)

You really can't go too far wrong with sincere words of thanks and gratitude. Make it a habit! My dad created a "thank-u-gram" using a cartoon of an old-fashioned telegram deliverer saying, "Have a happy day!" He printed them on inexpensive yellow paper, two to a sheet. Whenever he wanted to thank somebody, even for the smallest act of service or kindness, he was ready to go with a handwritten note and word of encouragement.

Create your own version of a thank-u-gram, or keep a supply of note cards on hand, just for such occasions. It doesn't have to be elaborate or lengthy. A thoughtful thank-you will always be gratefully received.

What Others Say: Quotes Worth Sharing

Feeling gratitude and not expressing it is like wrapping a present and not giving it.

William Arthur Ward

Gratitude is the memory of the heart.

Jean Baptiste Massieu

When we were children we were grateful to those who filled our stockings at Christmastime. Why are we not grateful to God for filling our stockings with legs?

G. K. Chesterton

I would maintain that thanks are the highest form of thought; and that gratitude is happiness doubled by wonder.

G. K. Chesterton

Who does not thank for little will not thank for much.

Estonian Proverb

Gratitude is the fairest blossom which springs from the soul.

Henry Ward Beecher

I can no other answer make, but, thanks, and thanks.

William Shakespeare

How far that little candle throws his beams!
So shines a good deed in a naughty world.

William Shakespeare,
Merchant of Venice

Kindness is the language which the deaf can hear and the blind can see.

Mark Twain

Scripture Passages to Read or Quote

I thank my God every time I remember you.

Philippians 1:3

First, I thank my God through Jesus Christ for all of you, because your faith is being reported all over the world. God, whom I serve in my spirit in preaching the gospel of his Son, is my witness how constantly I remember you in my prayers at all times.

Romans 1:8–10

Let the message of Christ dwell among you richly as you teach and admonish one another with all wisdom through psalms, hymns, and songs from the Spirit, singing to God with gratitude in your hearts.

Colossians 3:16

God loves a cheerful giver.

2 Corinthians 9:7

We ought always to thank God for you, brothers and sisters, and rightly so, because your faith is growing more and more, and the love all of you have for one another is increasing.

2 Thessalonians 1:3

Blessed are those who act justly, who always do what is right.

Psalm 106:3

May you be blessed by the LORD, the Maker of heaven and earth.

Psalm 115:15

The generous will themselves be blessed.

Proverbs 22:9

In everything I did, I showed you that by this kind of hard work we must help the weak, remembering the words the Lord Jesus himself said: "It is more blessed to give than to receive."

Acts 20:35

3

Words for the Sick and Suffering

"Get well soon!" There you go. It's a classic.
How many cards and letters have conveyed those three little words of cheer? A simple wish for better health, healing, and better days. But as with everything tried and true, the standard get-well wish could use a modern-day makeover.

One temptation in writing words of encouragement to somebody who is sick springs from a subconscious desire to resolve our own anxiety about that person's situation. The pain and uncertainty we feel for the seriously and chronically ill is something we want to be free of. Without being aware of it, we may add to a person's struggle by subtly demanding they get better so we can stop worrying about them.

It's not so hard to drop a line to a friend who's suffering a minor setback. But it's a lot harder to work through our feelings to craft a truly uplifting message for those walking through deep valleys because of illness or injury.

Here's an example from my own life. In 1995, our five-year-old son Chris was fighting for his life as he underwent weekly chemotherapy treatments for bone cancer. Imagine the challenge facing our friends as they tried to do and say the right things during one of the bleakest years my son Chris and our entire family has ever known.

Regular hospital visits an hour and a half away and frequent five-day stays dominated our lives. Twin brother Jon never knew which parent would be home to take care of him, but it was seldom both at once. When Chris was home, we couldn't go anywhere as a family because low white-cell counts made him vulnerable to germs of any kind. It was all we could do to manage Chris's medical crisis, get Jon to kindergarten, and still stay employed. We made it to church only sporadically. Days were a blur of exhaustion and uncertainty.

What kind of card do you send to a child who really doesn't grasp the seriousness of his illness? All he knows is that he's sick and his life is often miserable because of it. How do you encourage parents trying to keep it together, hoping all will be well, trusting God, but still constantly fearful?

Chris received a wide range of get-well wishes—everything from cards from friends of our parents all the way down the age-ladder to handwritten notes from other children. Some had stories; all tried to connect with him on his level.

All these years later, I dug out the basket of precious cards that came during that difficult time. See how vital these grace-filled words are? It's impossible to give them up; they were such a lifeline of hope.

If medals were awarded for courage, you would surely win one for patiently enduring all the treatments and hospital procedures. Jonathan should win a "best brother" award for supporting and encouraging you during your illness. When someone is sick, a loving, caring family is so important for recovery. We know that God is always watching over you and your family. With the doctors' help, you will soon be well and strong again. You are in our prayers.

(This note was sent with a teddy bear.) *We wanted you to know about a special friend of ours—someone as brave and as strong as you are—and how his bear has been his special friend during his care. A long time ago our friend Jack had some bad germs attack his heart. It was hard for Jack, and often he was alone. But someone gave Jack "Ted," and he didn't feel lonely so much. Ted became his special bear that went everywhere with him, especially to the hospital and for doctors' visits. One day, Jack got a new heart and Ted was there too! Ted was a good listener and he promised not to tell anyone anything Jack said. So they became best pals. We thought maybe this bear could become special to you. We send lots of love and good wishes, and look forward to more pictures of you and your brother as you continue to grow!*

(This note was written on a card with a picture of birds on the front. I love how the sender made a little story out of the drawing, bringing a smile to a sick little boy.) *Your grandparents told me about your illness and I'm very sorry about that. But the doctors know so much these days, I'm sure they will help you get well. Do you have little bluebirds like these to bring you your medicine, take your temperature, bring you a cracker, and take good care of you? It would be funny if birds took care of patients, wouldn't it?*

(This note came from a seven-year-old boy who was a leukemia survivor.) *I hope you get well soon. I can't wait till you do! Sincerely, Drew.* (The note is handwritten and illustrated with a picture of plants, Chris's favorite subject at the time.)

On a plain piece of paper, six-year-old Donny wrote: *Der Christopher I Hope tht you fel bter Love Donny.*

I'm teary all over again! What's common to these cards is that they reached out with a message of comfort and hope tailored to the receiver. There's another stack of cards to us, as parents needing understanding and offers of help and prayer. Each was an incredible blessing, bringing light to a very dark place.

Today, Chris is healthy and studying to be a doctor. His get-well cards have been in storage for fifteen years, but I think it's time to show them to him again. What a great way to learn empathy and bedside manner. It's all about putting yourself in someone else's place, even if that place is not a happy one.

Guidelines for Finding the Right Words

It can be hard to write a helpful note in a vacuum. Try to find out about the person's situation without intruding on his or her privacy. How did you learn about your friend or loved one's situation? Can you go back to that person or source to uncover details or get a recent report?

Sometimes in cases of serious injury or chronic or possibly terminal illness, the person or family sets up a website for periodic updates. Caringbridge.org is one of the most-often used sites. If you can find out from a family member about where to go for information, you'll be able to learn what you need to write a thoughtful note or letter.

No matter what the details of the person's situation are, you can write from your heart. Think about the things that are true: You care. God loves your friend or loved one. You will pray. You will be there.

You can include promises from God's Word and reminders of His power and love. See the Scripture passages included later in this chapter to help you get started.

What about the very difficult situation of someone who is dying? What can you say in that painful circumstance? A helpful answer comes in a letter from the "Ask Amy" column written by Amy Dickinson:

> *Dear Amy,*
>
> *I'd like to respond to "Marsha," who didn't know what to do for a friend who is dying of cancer.*
>
> *My brother recently died.*
>
> *I was most grateful for two letters from friends that he had the chance to read before his death.*
>
> *They reminded him of shared memories, highlighted his most special qualities and reiterated how much he meant to them. They said how much they loved him and how they would miss him. He shared them with me so proudly.*
>
> *—Another Reader*
>
> *Dear Reader,*
>
> *This sort of warmth and affection can be expressed even at a distance. Thank you.*[3]

Sometimes you are writing to acknowledge a temporary illness or a minor injury that has sidelined your friend, colleague, or relative. If the situation warrants it, a lighter approach may bring a smile and help the person focus on better days to come. You know the individual you are writing to and what might be appreciated most.

Just don't lean on clichés or pat answers to send your message. Be personal. Be real. Be specific.

Prompts to Help You Begin

In your scratch pad, jot down the name of the person you want to encourage and connect with. Write a few sentences or phrases describing what you know about the person's illness or injury.

Before going further, pause and pray for the person.

Try to put yourself in your friend or loved one's situation. Consider answers to the following questions, and write some ideas down in your notebook.

- What are some possible outcomes for this person?
- What is he or she likely experiencing right now?
- What fears might he or she have?
- What hopes might he or she have?
- What hopes do you hold for him or her?
- How did you pray for this person?

In your answers to the above questions, you may discover phrases and thoughts to include in your note of encouragement.

Read the Scripture passages at the end of this chapter, or seek God's Word on your own as you consider how He comforts us in times of struggle and pain.

Words to Make Your Own

When Someone Struggles With Short-Term Illness

- I was so sorry to hear about your illness. Please know I am praying for your swift and complete recovery.
- "And the God of all grace, who called you to his eternal glory in Christ, after you have suffered a little while, will himself restore you and make you strong, firm and steadfast. To him be the power for ever and ever" (1 Peter 5:10–11). May you find comfort in this promise today!
- Your co-workers are missing you and hoping for your restoration to full health very soon.
- We are praying that you will soon be well and able to return to your very busy life.
- This must be such a hard time for you and the family. Remember that you are loved! I trust you will be back to full health before long.

When Someone Suffers From a Chronic Illness

- May the Lord be your refuge in these difficult days.
- I pray that God's comfort will surround you as you seek answers for your illness.
- Please let me and others hold you up during this time of struggle. We truly want you to lean on us to help!
- How often I am reminded to pray for you as you battle your illness. May the prayers of the many who care for you give you hope and comfort.
- I hope these words from the psalmist will encourage you today: "He will cover you with his feathers, and under

his wings you will find refuge; his faithfulness will be your shield and rampart" (Psalm 91:4).

- God is great! Waiting on His blessings is hard. There seems not to be a "great day" on this earth, but there will be at His coming (and forever).

When Someone Is Struggling With a Terminal Illness

- During a time like this, I'm so thankful we can depend on the promises of Jesus: "My Father's house has many rooms; if that were not so, would I have told you that I am going there to prepare a place for you? And if I go and prepare a place for you, I will come back and take you to be with me that you also may be where I am" (John 14:2–3). Please know that you are loved.

- It's hard to know what to say right now. But I want you to know that I am praying for you and am so thankful for all you have contributed to my life.

- May God bring just the right comfort, just the right words, and the hope that only He can offer.

- Now we look through a glass darkly; one day we each will see Him face to face. I pray for you and your family in these days.

- Your life has been such a blessing to me. May God hold you in His hands and remind you that "all the days ordained for me were written in your book before one of them came to be" (Psalm 139:16).

- I have been holding you in my thoughts and my heart these days.

- May the God of peace surround you with His love and care, and may you truly experience the love of so many who are holding you up in prayer.

When Someone Is Recovering From an Injury

- "A cheerful heart is good medicine, but a crushed spirit dries up the bones" (Proverbs 17:22). If you need help cheering up, please let me know!
- I'm thinking of you often as you recover from your injury. Please know you are missed at work.
- The place just isn't the same without you; hurry back! Or take your time. Your choice.
- We were all so sorry to hear the bad news about your injury. May you find your way on the road to complete healing in the near future.
- I'm sure this is a painful and frustrating time for you. Please call me if I can bring over a meal or give you a ride anywhere.
- I was so sorry to learn about your injury! I know this will be a situation that God will oversee. But I'm here to help in any way I can. Just call me when you're ready!

When Someone Struggles With a Life-Altering Injury

- "Even though I walk through the darkest valley, I will fear no evil, for you are with me; your rod and your staff, they comfort me" (Psalm 23:4). These words of David remind us of God's care as a shepherd. May He comfort you today.
- News of your injury just arrived. We are so sorry to hear of all you have been through. Our prayers continue for all the strength the Lord can provide.
- Please know we are standing with you during this difficult time, and we want to do all we can to help.

Aunt Me-me's Guide to What *Not* to Say

Aunt Me-me believes she is a terrific people person, and in her enthusiasm, she sometimes makes false assumptions. These result in words that aren't always helpful, as the following examples illustrate.

I bet you can't wait to get out of that cast and back onto the slopes. (What if the person sustained such a bad injury, he or she has been advised to never ski again? Perhaps there is unresolved grief, and being reminded of the loss isn't helpful.)

Now don't just lie around moping. I'll be over to get you out of the house in the next week! I'm sure the mall has missed us! (What if the person is depressed about the injury or illness, but still needs rest and quiet? Is shopping therapy really the best cure?)

I had that same surgery, and I know just what you're going through. I'm sure you'll bounce right back, just like I did! (What if the recovery is sidetracked? Don't diminish what others are going through or put too much emphasis on your own experience.)

If you really have faith, God will heal you. I'm praying for your complete recovery. (Wow, this opens up a whole can of theological worms. It's better not to make promises on God's behalf, especially in the case of chronic or potentially terminal illnesses. Let God be in charge of the outcome, and focus on His promises of comfort and love.)

I do want to help during this time. What can I do? (Use your imagination and personal experience when it comes to offers of help. Think of something specific, such as bringing a meal or cleaning the house. Offer that service, with easy contact information so your friend or loved one can reach you at the appropriate time. Find ways to help without making the sick person come up with all the ideas.)

I feel so terrible about your accident! Why did this have to happen to you? I wake up each day wondering how God could have allowed this in your life. (Don't burden the sick or injured person with your own pain or doubts about their suffering. That just makes them feel worse, or forces them to think up ways to comfort you! You need to carry the weight in this case and find ways to lighten the other person's load of care.)

I am so sorry to hear you have cancer! I lost a dear friend to that same cancer, but I know you have what it takes to beat it. (People with serious illnesses don't want to hear about others who didn't make it. While you don't want to gloss over the seriousness of the illness, keep your tone hopeful and focus on positive messages.)

What Others Say: Quotes Worth Sharing

Hope is the thing with feathers, that perches in the soul, and sings the tune without words, and never stops at all.

Emily Dickinson

Hope is the last thing ever lost.

Italian Proverb

Consult not your fears but your hopes and your dreams. Think not about your frustrations, but about your unfulfilled potential. Concern yourself not with what you tried and failed in, but with what it is still possible for you to do.

Pope John XXIII

Hope is putting faith to work when doubting would be easier.

Anonymous

Faith is like radar that sees through the fog—the reality of things at a distance that the human eye cannot see.

Corrie ten Boom

Sorrow looks back, worry looks around, faith looks up.

Quoted in *Guideposts* magazine

There is one thing which gives radiance to everything. It is the idea of something around the corner.

G. K. Chesterton

For happiness one needs security, but joy can spring like a flower even from the cliffs of despair.

Anne Morrow Lindbergh

Scripture Passages to Read or Quote

My son, pay attention to what I say;
   turn your ear to my words.
Do not let them out of your sight,
   keep them within your heart;
for they are life to those who find them
   and health to one's whole body.

Proverbs 4:20–22

LORD my God, I called to you for help,
   and you healed me.

Psalm 30:2

Whoever dwells in the shelter of the Most High
   will rest in the shadow of the Almighty.

I will say of the LORD, "He is my refuge and my
   fortress,
   my God, in whom I trust."
                                        Psalm 91:1–2

Though the fig tree does not bud
   and there are no grapes on the vines,
though the olive crop fails
   and the fields produce no food,
though there are no sheep in the pen
   and no cattle in the stalls,
yet I will rejoice in the LORD,
   I will be joyful in God my Savior.
                                        Habakkuk 3:17–18

The Sovereign LORD is my strength;
   he makes my feet like the feet of a deer,
   he enables me to tread on the heights.
                                        Habakkuk 3:19

But I will sing of your strength,
   in the morning I will sing of your love;
for you are my fortress,
   my refuge in times of trouble.

You are my strength, I sing praise to you;
   you, God, are my fortress,
   my God on whom I can rely.
                                        Psalm 59:16–17

I said, "Oh, that I had the wings of a dove!
   I would fly away and be at rest.
I would flee far away
   and stay in the desert;

I would hurry to my place of shelter,
    far from the tempest and storm."
                        Psalm 55:6–8

My comfort in my suffering is this:
    Your promise preserves my life.
                        Psalm 119:50

For no one is cast off
    by the Lord forever.
Though he brings grief, he will show compassion,
    so great is his unfailing love.
For he does not willingly bring affliction
    or grief to anyone.
                        Lamentations 3:31–33

Do not let your hearts be troubled.
                        John 14:1

Even though I walk
    through the darkest valley,
I will fear no evil,
    for you are with me;
your rod and your staff,
    they comfort me.
                        Psalm 23:4

I will not leave you as orphans; I will come to you.
                        John 14:18

He pierced my heart
    with arrows from his quiver . . .
So I say, "My splendor is gone
    and all that I had hoped from the LORD." . . .

Yet this I call to mind
and therefore I have hope:
Because of the LORD's great love we are not
consumed,
for his compassions never fail.

Lamentations 3:13, 18, 21–22

4

Words for Birthdays

Birthday celebrations and wishes are deeply embedded in our culture. Did you know that people have been sending birthday cards for more than a hundred years? We have parties, eat cake, light candles, make wishes, give presents, yell "surprise," and sometimes even wear those funny, pointed paper hats.

Why all the hoopla? We recognize birthdays as opportunities to affirm each individual as a unique human being, generally one we are thankful to have in our lives. And as believers, we can bring even more depth to an annual birthday wish, and turn it into an occasion to fulfill the biblical mandate to care for one another and esteem others more highly than ourselves.

We read in Galatians, "Let us not become weary in doing good, for at the proper time we will reap a harvest if we do not give up. Therefore, as we have opportunity, let us do good to all people, especially to those who belong to the family of believers" (Galatians 6:9–10). Now, sending a birthday greeting may seem like a fairly simple, even mundane means of "doing good." But what if you really took time to think about what the birthday celebrant means to you and shared that in a thoughtful message?

Facebook has made the whole process of sending birthday messages into a streamlined, Internet-enabled cinch. First, your Facebook home page lists all your friends' birthdays every day, but if you fail to notice, you'll likely see all your other friends writing on the birthday friend's Wall. Quickly, you react and try to phrase a short message that isn't an exact copy of the fifty messages already there. It's the thought that counts, right?

And Twitter? I guess I'm flattered that my tweeting son, who somehow has garnered more than three thousand Twitter followers, used his 140 characters one day to wish me happy birthday in front of his world. I'm glad that for a few seconds, they all realized I'm the "best mom ever." And maybe for a twenty-one-year-old guy, that's the best I can expect. But it does seem to require minimum effort. After all, as I like to remind him, "I gave you life!"

Social networking is a big time-saver: No more driving to the store, flipping through card after card to find one that's funny or beautiful or age-targeted. No more hunting for a mailing address. No more planning more than a day ahead.

But what we've gained in promptness, we've lost in personalization. Stop and think about how special you feel when you receive a card or note in the mail with handwritten thoughts expressing just why you are so special. Maybe there's a little enclosure. Not just a check from Grandma, but maybe a bookmark, a photo, or a clipping that conveys, "I thought of you." That's more than a "Happy Birthday." That's a blessing.

Among the many definitions of the word *bless* are these: to wish good for, to feel grateful to, to make happy or fortunate. I especially like the idea of a birthday wish that includes what I hope for a person combined with my gratitude about having that person in my life. This chapter has some ideas to help you go the extra mile and turn a simple "Happy Birthday" into a message that uplifts, encourages, and blesses.

Guidelines for Finding the Right Words

Let's start with this powerful guideline to lead our thoughts about the subject of blessing others from Philippians 4:8–9:

> Finally, brothers and sisters, whatever is true, whatever is noble, whatever is right, whatever is pure, whatever is lovely, whatever is admirable—if anything is excellent or praiseworthy—think about such things. Whatever you have learned or received or heard from me, or seen in me—put it into practice. And the God of peace will be with you.

So focus on the person with the birthday. What can you say to that person that will be true, admirable, or praiseworthy? How can you let him or her know what he or she has contributed to your life? Of course, your message will be determined by the age of the recipient and the kind of relationship you have. But don't let another year go by where you simply sign a card and leave it at that.

Remember how exciting a birthday is for a child. I love to recall how crazy our household was on the day of our twins' birthdays each year as they grew up. Though every year the party was much the same (pizza, two cakes, friends over for food and games), the thrill built from year to year. When the boys reached their teens and the gifts switched from toys to cash, I was sure they considered their birthdays to be the biggest fund-raiser of the year. They pooled their money and bought video games from a list compiled for months beforehand and ranked in priority order.

When it comes to birthday wishes, what delights children hasn't changed much over the years. One vintage card, illustrated with a cute puppy, has this timeless verse:

> *Here's a friendly little puppy.*
> *If he could talk he'd say,*
> *"Here are 3 birthday wishes,*
> *because you're 3 today."*

In his mouth, the puppy holds a cardboard sign listing the wishes: 1) Good times; 2) Surprises; 3) Friends to play with. Many decades later, those three wishes still apply to children.

Of course, it's different for adults. The year my mom turned seventy, she commented a bit wistfully, "Well, it's not like I wake up and say, 'Yay, it's my birthday.'" And as we grow older, our birthdays take on different colors depending on the year we just survived and the year we expect to face. These milestones can bring great joy, or they can be bittersweet. That's why a message of love, care, and affirmation can mean even more as the years go by.

The "Prompts to Help You Begin" section includes a variety of ideas and starters to help you craft a memorable, meaningful birthday message. Be sure to read the Scripture quotes too, for inspiration or to include as blessings in the cards you send.

You might find it helpful to semi-automate your birthday greeting process by picking out cards once or twice a year and having them ready to go when the time comes. At the start of the year, put your birthday reminder dates into a calendar or computer file. At the end of each month, locate addresses for those celebrating birthdays in the month to come. Address your cards and pencil in the birthdays in the upper right corner (where a stamp will later cover your reminder). Mail a week before the date.

Here are some ideas of things to tuck into cards for gifts: bookmarks, stamps, postcards, photos, newspaper clippings, recipes, and the ever-popular gift cards or checks.

There's nothing wrong with sending personalized e-cards via email, or sending a thoughtful message via email, maybe one with a link to a pertinent web article, birthday history, or photo. It still beats that last-minute "Oh yeah, have a great birthday" on Facebook or Twitter.

In spite of the speed and immediacy offered by the Internet, I still prefer the impact of a handwritten, snail-mailed card with a thoughtful, personal message included. In fact, you can even skip the card; just send me a note that's all about me.

Prompts to Help You Begin

- What kind of year has the person you are celebrating just come through? How might that inform the message you want to write?
- If you are writing to a child, list the child's main interests. How can you weave those into your message? Can you include something in the card that reflects a major interest? Or just choose a card that shows cars, dinosaurs, dolls, or something else the child enjoys.

- What are some major passions of the person you are writing to? Do any of those lend themselves to positive metaphors or comparisons? For example, to a hiker: "May the year ahead offer you incredible views as you conquer every peak." Or a golfer: "I wish you a year filled with success and some holes-in-one you never expected." Use your scratch pad to play around with some metaphor ideas.
- Write down at least one personal memory you share with the birthday person. How can you refer to that happy memory in your message?
- Why is the birthday person special to you? State that in very straightforward language.

Words to Make Your Own

Here are sample birthday wishes to adapt or use as models for your own.

Birthday Wishes for Friends

- On this special occasion of your birthday, I remember how truly thankful I am for our friendship.
- I'm so glad you were born! You bring great joy to all around you, especially me. Thank you for being my friend.
- May God bless you with hope and joy as you meet another year with your usual energy and optimism.
- Now that a difficult year has passed, may your birthday mark the start of better days ahead.

- You are an amazing person. How blessed the world is because you are in it. May God grant you a wonderful year ahead.
- Not really counting the years, but counting our blessings and all the happy memories our friendship has brought. God bless you on your birthday!
- Another birthday has rolled around, and another reason to celebrate the special gifts you bring to the world.

Birthday Wishes for Colleagues

- I hope your birthday is full of reminders of how much people care about you.
- Happy birthday! This place wouldn't be the same without you.
- You give so much to everything you do. May this birthday find you filled with energy and excitement for the year ahead.
- You take the cake. Seriously. It's your birthday, so take the cake! And thanks for sharing the way you do.
- Your birthday is a reminder that I am so fortunate to get to work with you. Thanks for the leadership you model for all of us.
- May God grant you another great year of growing, learning, and contributing to our lives here at work.
- Happy birthday, and thanks for making work fun. Well, at least fun-ish.
- Best wishes on your birthday. Enjoy this celebration of you!
- Here's hoping your birthday is almost as special as you are.

Birthday Wishes for Neighbors

- When I think about good neighbors, I think about you and am thankful. Have a great birthday celebration!
- Since it's your birthday, I wanted to thank you for all you bring to the neighborhood. Have a great year ahead!
- What is it about birthdays that make us count our blessings? I hope you are counting yours. Know that you are a blessing in my life.
- One thing we can count on each year: a birthday. And thanks for letting me count on you, neighbor.
- May you have a birthday filled with fun, friends, and great memories. I'm so glad you are part of our neighborhood.

Birthday Wishes for Family Members

- May this birthday remind you of how much I love you.
- You bring so much to my life and to our entire family. May God bless you with a wonderful birthday and year ahead.
- It hasn't been the easiest year, but I pray that this birthday marks a new beginning and sunnier days to come.
- You have always been a wonderful contributor to my life. Your birthday is the perfect time to tell you again how much I thank you.
- As another year comes and goes, you remain the heart of our family. Thank you for all you do, and may God bless you with great joy.
- No family is complete without someone like you! Have a happy and memorable birthday!

birthday cards. When someone is struggling, that "hilarious" card just may evoke real tears of sadness instead of the tears of laughter Me-me was going for.

Another no-no illustrated by Aunt Me-me involves inappropriate humor. She loves to choose cards that imply a birthday is just a big excuse for wild excess, heavy drinking, and crazy partying. But the young people she sends those to actually hold higher values and find themselves offended instead of affirmed. Or she picks out "funny" cards with crude or demeaning illustrations and photos. They make her laugh in the card shop, but there's a good chance these tacky choices won't be saved or valued, and may end up being pitched instead of proudly displayed.

Humor itself isn't a bad thing. In fact, the perfect funny card gives the gift of laughter and conveys shared history and understanding. But do be careful to pick a card that really reflects the person receiving it and the relationship you share. If you think there's a chance the person will get the wrong message or won't get the joke at all, choose another card—one that's positive and cheering. Don't let the warmth of your message get lost because you're looking for cheap laughs.

What Others Say: Quotes Worth Sharing

It's not the years in your life but the life in your years that counts.

Adlai Stevenson

The great thing about getting older is that you don't lose all the other ages you've been.

Madeleine L'Engle

Just remember, once you're over the hill, you begin to pick up speed.

Charles Schulz

One advantage in growing older is that you can stand for more and fall for less.

Monta Crane

Wisdom doesn't necessarily come with age. Sometimes age just shows up all by itself.

Tom Wilson

When I was younger, I could remember anything, whether it had happened or not.

Mark Twain

May the road rise up to meet you.
May the wind be always at your back.
May the sun shine warm upon your face;
And the rains fall soft upon your fields
And until we meet again,
May God hold you in the palm of His hand.

Traditional Gaelic Blessing

May you always have work for your hands to do.
May your pockets hold always a coin or two.
May the sun shine bright on your windowpane.
May the rainbow be certain to follow each rain.
May the hand of a friend always be near you.
And may God fill your heart with gladness to cheer you.

Irish Blessing

Scripture Passages to Read or Quote

Let love and faithfulness never leave you;
bind them around your neck,
write them on the tablet of your heart.
Then you will win favor and a good name
in the sight of God and man.

Proverbs 3:3–4

Now may the God of peace, who through the blood of the eternal covenant brought back from the dead our Lord Jesus, that great Shepherd of the sheep, equip you with everything good for doing his will, and may he work in us what is pleasing to him, through Jesus Christ, to whom be glory for ever and ever. Amen.

Hebrews 13:20–21

But do not forget this one thing, dear friends: With the Lord a day is like a thousand years, and a thousand years are like a day.

2 Peter 3:8

The LORD bless you
and keep you;
the LORD make his face shine on you
and be gracious to you;
the LORD turn his face toward you
and give you peace.

Numbers 6:24–26

And God is able to bless you abundantly, so that in all things at all times, having all that you need, you will abound in every good work.

2 Corinthians 9:8

The Lord be with your spirit. Grace be with you all.

2 Timothy 4:22

May you be blessed by the LORD,
the Maker of heaven and earth.

Psalm 115:15

Therefore we do not lose heart. Though outwardly we are wasting away, yet inwardly we are being renewed day by day.

2 Corinthians 4:16

And I pray that you, being rooted and established in love, may have power, together with all the Lord's holy people, to grasp how wide and long and high and deep is the love of Christ, and to know this love that surpasses knowledge—that you may be filled to the measure of all the fullness of God.

Ephesians 3:17–19

5

Words for Weddings and Engagements

Whether one is getting engaged or getting married, the age-old process of two becoming one has morphed from the very simple ("The preacher's free next Sunday; we're gettin' hitched!") to the unbelievably complex.

Which is why this chapter is going to focus on the words and only the words, including what to say on invitations and announcements as well as how to congratulate the couple. If you're looking for the *Etiquette-ly Accurate Guide to All Things Wedding Related,* I believe you'll want to spend some time in your local bookstore or with your favorite search engine.

But the words alone and the best way to avoid wedding-related disasters still make a substantial meal for this little chapter. How so? Well, let's just consider a few stunning "fails" chronicled on one website.

- I once received a wedding invitation to a ceremony in Las Vegas. I don't live too far from Vegas, so I thought it might be fun to go—until I got to the bottom of the invitation, where the bride and groom listed a bank account number into which guests could make direct fund transfers from their own bank to the happy couple's new joint account. Needless to say, I didn't attend the wedding, nor did I send a "gift."

- My boyfriend and I were invited to his friend's wedding. The invitation was handwritten on what appeared to be plain white printer paper. Okay, so they didn't have a lot of money to spare. However, written at the bottom of the invitation were the words: "Price of dinner: $20.00 per person." We were expected to pay for our own dinner! I told my boyfriend that that was the tackiest thing I'd ever seen.

- My husband's brother is getting married in about a month, and the invitation seems to be one etiquette nightmare after another.
  1. We were given our invitations in person, apparently to save on postage.
  2. Inside the invitation is a card that reads, "In lieu of a traditional wedding gift, the bride and groom request checks toward their honeymoon cruise." This was followed by their travel agent's name and address, and a statement saying that a copy of the check would be retained for the bride and groom's reference.
  3. Although the bride and groom requested money in place of gifts, just in case, they included a second card that gave us the FIVE locations at which they registered.

4. Last but certainly not least, when I went to mail back our RSVP, I noticed that it had no stamp. I had to stamp it in order to get it back to them by the deadline. We're very tempted to get nothing at all or something not on their registry. (Did I mention they registered at FIVE locations?) However, one bad turn does not deserve another. We do refuse, however, to send cash.

- My brother's wedding was two years ago, and he asked me how to word the invitation. Our dad's been dead for fourteen years, but my brother wanted Dad's name mentioned on the invitation. I told him to say, "Bob Smith, son of Mary Smith and the late John Smith, and Janey Jones, daughter of Mr. and Mrs. Davey Jones, request the pleasure of your company . . . " Instead he wrote, "Mary Smith and the late John Smith and Mr. and Mrs. Davey Jones request the pleasure of your company at the marriage of their children." I ask you, how can my father invite someone from beyond the grave? I cringed when I read this.[4]

Announcing an Engagement When It's Fairly Simple

Here, the "how" is often more complicated than "what" to say. This is a good subject for etiquette books and websites. Yet I do submit for your consideration this question: Should you announce your engagement on Facebook?

This short excerpt from a web article by Maura Kelly may enlighten you about the issues:

A woman I usually quite like recently posted perhaps the most annoying update of all: "I can't believe I'm smiling down at the pretty new ring on my finger . . ."

As if it weren't bad enough that she was having success in a relationship, whereas I never do, add to that the *coyness*! The 765 nearly identical gurgling congratulatory responses! All the exclamation points!!!

There was also the friend of a friend who announced her future wedding thusly: "Woo-hoo! I'm engaged! I figured it would happen soon, but I didn't realize it would happen THIS WEEKEND!"

That one made me wonder how many Facebook friends she lost as she gained a fiancé. . . . The outright bragging might be even more offensive than the not-so-sly reference to the ring. . . .

I understand the impulse to announce your happy moment on Facebook—you want to celebrate and you also want to announce the news without making 765 phone calls. But for the record, please let me say: THERE'S A RIGHT WAY AND A WRONG WAY TO ANNOUNCE ON FACEBOOK THAT YOU'RE GETTING HITCHED. So please, simply change your relationship status to "engaged" and be done with it.[5]

Facebook's not the only game in town. There are other ways to announce engagements—some formal, some not so much. There are handwritten letters to family and friends with a projected wedding date; printed save-the-date cards; announcements in the hometown newspaper; formal printed engagement announcements; or a special party or other event where the happy news is shared. You could post a video on YouTube and send out a link.

Soon-to-be-marrieds have many more options these days. They just need to make it special and tailor it to their unique personalities and lives. Or just update their Facebook status.

Wedding Invitations 101

Two words suffice for all wedding-related correspondence: *courtesy* and *common sense*. Three words. Well . . . *courtesy*, *common sense*, and *care*. Four. That's four words.

Styles and approaches to wedding invitations are as varied as the personalities of couples getting married. But here are a few basics that will help when it comes to finding the right words.

Wedding invitations can be engraved, printed, electronic, or handwritten, but the more formal the wedding, the more formal the invitations.

Formal invitations have two envelopes and include enclosures such as maps, RSVP cards, and envelopes. For a small, casual wedding, handwrite invitations on good-quality notepaper, print invitations on a home computer, or use an evite.

Be sure invitations include:

- Names of bride and groom
- Date and time
- Location
- Mention of reception to follow, if any
- Expression of pleasure at having guests celebrate with you
- Request for a response and a way to respond (RSVP)

The invitation may be issued by the couple, by both their parents, by the woman's parents, by the man's parents, or by a relative or family friend—whoever is hosting the event or whatever is most appropriate.

A deceased person may be included if the invitation is sent by the bride and groom: "Lily Ross, daughter of Betsy Ross and the late George Ross, and Jedidiah Smith, son of Mr. and Mrs. John Smith, request the honor of your presence . . ."

Engagement Announcements and Wedding Invitations 202

In a time with a declining number of traditional, nuclear family units, it's not uncommon to have multiple sets of parents or even grandparents involved in planning a wedding. The addition of multiple sets of parents can make things more complicated.

Solutions and answers exist, but the best piece of advice for relatives to remember is that the bride and groom's happiness should be the central focus for everyone involved. If relatives heed that advice and maintain a positive, cooperative attitude, logistics will have a way of working out. Of course, the couple getting married needs to focus outward at the same time, and keep family dynamics in mind with sensitivity and caring.

In the case of blended families, the bride and groom might begin by considering their relationship with each set of parents and stepparents. They can start by opening the lines of communication early in the process, to set a good tone. The bride and groom may want to sit down and talk with all their parents and sort out how they feel and what makes them comfortable. Many potentially uncomfortable situations can be headed off by early discussion.

Usually the parents who raised the child (bride or groom) will be most involved in helping to plan the wedding. If both sets of parents raised the child, then the child and all her or his parents will want to discuss and divide the responsibilities and coordinate activities.

Today's young couples often avoid this problem completely by taking charge of and planning their own weddings. While this may cut back on stress, it seems unfortunate to keep parents out of the joyful time that wedding planning can be.

The engagement announcement is usually made by the parents with whom the bride has lived most of her life. Here are two approaches for wording these announcements:

- "Mrs. Mary Jones announces the engagement of her daughter Matilda to . . ."
- In other situations, both the bride's parents are mentioned. The announcement can read, "Mrs. Mary Jones of Conifer and Mr. Jim Smith of Pine announce the engagement of their daughter Matilda to . . ."

The wording of wedding invitations becomes more sensitive when there are multiple sets of parents. There are a variety of solutions.

- One way to avoid the debate about who announces the wedding on the invitation is for the couple to do it themselves. For example: "Together with our parents, we request the honor of your presence at . . ."
- Generally the invitation will include either both sets of parents' names or neither. Should both parents or either parent be remarried, but the bride and groom do not wish to include stepparents in the invitation, it may read "Mrs. Betsy Ross and Mr. Alexander Hamilton request the honor of your presence at the wedding of their daughter . . ."
- If only one parent and stepparent are announcing the wedding, the wording should indicate whose child is

being married. For instance, "Mr. and Mrs. John Smith request the honor of your presence at the wedding of Mrs. Smith's daughter . . ."

- If both parents have remarried and are hosting the wedding jointly, both names should be listed on the invitation, with the mother of the bride listed first. It may read: "Mr. and Mrs. Betsy Ross and Mr. and Mrs. Alexander Hamilton request the honor of your presence at the wedding of their daughter Lily Hamilton to . . ."

Words for Wedding Announcements

Wedding announcements are sent to those who weren't invited to the ceremony or reception, using the same model as the invitations. Announcements can be worded in several ways, including:

- From the bride's family: "Mr. and Mrs. XX announce the marriage of their daughter XX to . . ."
- From the couple themselves: "[Bride's name] and [groom's name] announce their marriage on Saturday, the sixth of June . . ."
- From both sets of parents: "XX and XX and YY and YY announce the marriage of their daughter and son, ZX and ZY, on Saturday, the sixth of June, two thousand and twelve, First Baptist Church, Pine, Colorado."

Announcements should be mailed out as near to the wedding date as possible, and may include at-home cards with the couple's current address.

Words for Reply Cards

Wedding RSVP etiquette is very simple when it comes to the wording on the cards. The simpler the card, the easier it will be for the guest to respond quickly. The bride and groom should include a self-addressed and stamped envelope for the guest to return the RSVP card.

RSVP Card Ideas

M _____

will _____ attend.

Name _____

Number Attending _____

Unable to Attend _____

The favor of your reply is requested by January 1, 2012.

M _____

_____ Accepts with pleasure

_____ Declines with regrets

We look forward to celebrating your wedding with you.

M _____

_____ accepts _____ regrets

85

We have reserved two seats in your honor.
Please respond by January 1, 2012.

M _____

_____ Accepts with pleasure _____ Declines with regrets

M _____

_____ is looking forward to celebrating with you
_____ regretfully will not be able to

Words for Responding to the Couple

With today's plethora of cell phones, smartphones, and texting options, plus email, evites, and a world of social media, responding to an invitation offers as many choices as technology can create to torture us. Fortunately, most formal wedding invitations come with delightful RSVP cards for the guest to use when responding. If this isn't the case, do your best to respond in kind: evite to evite, text to text. Whatever you do, respond.

When you are invited to share in a wedding celebration, courtesy requires you to respond quickly, even if you will not attend. It's as simple as that. In most cases, the wedding invitation will include a self-addressed, stamped envelope. This makes it easy to sign your name, indicate if you will or will not be attending, and send the RSVP card back.

Words to Bless the Couple

A wedding or engagement is a wonderful occasion to express your positive thoughts and feelings about the person getting married, or the couple if you know both parties well. Think about including a little story from the past, an example of the couple's love for each other, encouragement for the future, and even a few words of advice, as long as they aren't heavy-handed.

Here are some examples to get you started:

- As you launch your lives together, I pray God will give you His joy, peace, and guidance through all the years to come.

- May you find great happiness together, contributing to each other's strengths and sharing your love through all of life's challenges and changes.

- I remember the first time I saw you as a couple. The energy you two share could power an airplane! May you fly together on the wings of the wind.

- As an old married person, I know what it takes to stay together during thick and thin. You two have what it takes, and I'm so proud of you today!

- May you grow together from this day forward, now one, united in God's love and surrounded by those who love you.

- Your wedding is such a wonderful example of love's triumph and the joy of commitment in an uncertain world. Your future is bright because you know the Author of tomorrow.

- May you experience God's blessings today and through the years. And know that I plan to be there for both of you, to share my support and encouragement as the years go by.

Talking Points: What to Say in a Wedding Receiving Line

Not all weddings feature a receiving line these days, but many do as a way of ensuring that the bride, groom, and key family and friends have an opportunity to greet each guest. Here the need for warmth and sincerity is trumped only by the need to keep it short and sweet. People are behind you in the line and possibly more than a little hungry for some cake.

You can't go far wrong if you stay on the side of simplicity, though you may want to be aware of an old tradition holding that you say "congratulations" to the groom only, while the bride receives your "best wishes." Apparently "congratulations" could imply a prize won or that you caught something. The old-school thinking was that while the groom won a prize, the bride wasn't out trying to "catch her man," and saying congratulations could insult her with the idea that she bagged him! Still, if you slip up and say congratulations to the bride, she's probably unaware of this past practice and will happily accept your congrats.

When you move through the line, shake hands (or kiss/hug the bride if appropriate), say your greetings, and move along. You may need to offer a very succinct introduction to those in the party who don't really know you. "Hi, I'm (name), and I work with (bride or groom)/went to school with/met the bride and groom at Bible study," etc.

Here are a few other ideas. Remember, you aren't being graded on originality, but on your sincerity and enthusiasm!

- Thanks so much for inviting me to the wedding.
- You look so wonderful and happy!
- That was a lovely/moving/inspiring ceremony.
- May God bless you throughout your life together.

- (You may want to compliment something specific about the wedding, such as the music, the flowers, the setting, etc.)

Aunt Me-me's Guide to What *Not* to Say

Aunt Me-me was married a few years ago. Apparently she felt that consulting etiquette guides was for amateurs (after all, it was her third time around). Based on my observations, here are her top seven wedding blunders. Not that I would point them out to her or anything. That would be rude.

1. Her invitation mentioned the money tree that would be at the reception. With a suggested donation amount.
2. She sent out certain invitations after the wedding. While claiming they got lost in the mail is a somewhat believable excuse, it's an inexcusable way to save money on reception catering.
3. She included a return envelope intended for monetary gifts. And it wasn't even stamped.
4. Her RSVP cards were blank. While her guests should feel complimented that she thought they were bright enough to know what to do, she was disappointed when she received several envelopes containing blank cards.
5. She sent me a pity invite. If someone receives an invitation to your wedding within two weeks of the actual event, they are going to know that you pity-invited them.
6. She called my significant other "and guest" when she had already met that "guest" at least twice.
7. She was sad her late parents wouldn't be able to attend her latest wedding. Instead of honoring them in the wedding program, during a wedding toast, or on

the wedding website, she chose the from-the-grave approach with this wording: "Luigi (deceased) and Fifi (also deceased) Beebe invite you to attend the wedding of their daughter Me-me . . ."

What Others Say: Quotes Worth Sharing

May God be with you and bless you.
May you see your children's children.
May you be poor in misfortune, rich in blessings.
May you know nothing but happiness
From this day forward.

An Old Wedding Blessing

Marriage should be a duet—when one sings, the other claps.

Joe Murray

Marriage is like vitamins: We supplement each other's minimum daily requirements.

Kathy Mohnke

A good marriage is like an incredible retirement fund. You put everything you have into it during your productive life, and over the years it turns from silver to gold to platinum.

Willard Scott, *The Joy of Living*

In marriage, being the right person is as important as finding the right person.

Wilbert Donald Gough

Chains do not hold a marriage together. It is threads, hundreds of tiny threads, which sew people together through the years.

Simone Signoret

The goal in marriage is not to think alike, but to think together.

Robert C. Dodds

Married life teaches one invaluable lesson: to think of things far enough ahead not to say them.

Jefferson Machamer

Scripture Passages to Read or Quote

Love is patient, love is kind. It does not envy, it does not boast, it is not proud. It does not dishonor others, it is not self-seeking, it is not easily angered, it keeps no record of wrongs. Love does not delight in evil but rejoices with the truth. It always protects, always trusts, always hopes, always perseveres . . . And now these three remain: faith, hope and love. But the greatest of these is love.

1 Corinthians 13:4–7, 13

"Haven't you read," [Jesus] replied, "that at the beginning the Creator 'made them male and female,' and said, 'For this reason a man will leave his father and mother and be united to his wife, and the two will become one flesh'? So they are no longer two, but one flesh. Therefore what God has joined together, let no one separate."

Matthew 19:4–6

Follow God's example, therefore, as dearly loved children and walk in the way of love, just as Christ loved us and gave himself up for us as a fragrant offering and sacrifice to God.

Ephesians 5:1–2

91

A wife of noble character who can find? She is worth far more than rubies.

Proverbs 31:10

May your fountain be blessed, and may you rejoice in the wife of your youth.

Proverbs 5:18

6

Words of Encouragement

Carry each other's burdens, and in this way you will fulfill the law of Christ.

Galatians 6:2

A while ago, I found myself emailing in the middle of the night with a woman who's been a dear friend since college. It was a night neither of us could sleep for various reasons, but mostly involving worries about our adult children and choices they were making at the time.

When my friend wrote to comfort and encourage me, I found her note to be a wonderful model of words that are helpful during these times.

I care about you and your broken heart.

Remember that your kids belong to God. They are the precious lost sheep that the Lord has gone out to rescue and bring safely back into the fold.

I pray for God's protection for my "lost sheep" every morning, knowing that God is caring for them and is holding them in His everlasting arms of love. Our Lord cares for His lost sheep even more than all the rest. Your children have been dedicated to God and they are His forever, especially during times of greatest emotional pain.

As a mom, I do feel your pain, and I will be praying and asking Jesus to intercede for them to the Father who loves our children, just as He loves His own Son . . . our dear savior.

Why was this note so effective? For several reasons.

First, my friend reminded me about the strength of our friendship and stated that she cared about me, not just generally, but at this unique time and in this specific situation.

Then she reminded me of a reassuring truth: My children belong to God, and He loves them greatly.

Next, she described her own actions and identified her needs with my own, illustrating again how she is leaning on God's truth in this hard time. She knows my feelings because hers are so similar.

Finally, she promises to act—to pray with hope and expectation, based on God's love and care.

My friend is not a professional writer. But her words were filled with grace and met my need for encouragement in the best way. She didn't minimize the situation or downplay my feelings or hers. She is real, transparent, and vulnerable. If encouragement is at all about coming alongside, my good friend knows how to do that, even at three o'clock in the morning.

Guidelines for Finding the Right Words

Many of the principles from chapter 1, "Words for the Grieving," apply here. When you want to encourage someone who is struggling through a difficult time, you have to enter into

94

that person's experience. You need to make an effort to think about their feelings and fears. And that can be a little intimidating, especially if your own life seems to be a lot happier in comparison. I mean, isn't it harder to comfort a friend who just got laid off when you're working comfortably in secure employment?

It can hurt to hurt for our friends and family members. But this small sacrifice is what Jesus modeled and calls us to.

Read through some of the Scripture passages at the end of this chapter, and let them guide your thoughts and attitudes about encouragement. The Bible is filled with wonderful stories and examples of those who cared for others in need. Take time to be inspired before you begin.

You may want to rifle through your own collection of cards you've been sent through the years. Maybe you're not a saver like me, but I have files filled with handwritten notes and cards from friends and family members who touched my life when I needed it most. That's what's so great about hard-copy communications. They can sit in a drawer for years, but still speak to you when you need them to.

Don't forget to offer a listening ear. Encouragement isn't just about telling. It's about understanding what the other person is going through and letting him or her be honest about the whole experience. If you send a note, consider a specific invitation to get together for coffee or a walk, so you can talk and pray together.

Prompts to Help You Begin

- Before you start, think about some specific needs your friend or family member is facing. You may know

95

something about the person's loss or struggle, but try to identify what needs have arisen because of it. Pray about how you might meet that need, starting with your words of care and concern.

- In order to be sensitive to the person you are writing to, think about your own history. Have you lost a job? A love? A dream? Take a few minutes to jot down two or three sentences expressing what you felt at the time. These memories and scribblings can help you craft a message that is honest and helpful too.

- As you remember a time when you were struggling, try to recall what specific help or words were really useful in dealing with your pain. If you do have a collection of notes and cards, look through them for examples of messages that inspired you and comforted you. Or try to recall why some people truly gave you assistance while others just added to your despair.

- Here are some feelings the person you are writing to may be experiencing: isolation, fear, helplessness, loss of self-worth, anxiety, or even anger.

Words to Make Your Own

A Job Loss

- I'm so sorry to hear you lost your job. Please know that I'll be praying for you and want to help you in any way I can. If there's any networking assistance I can give, please let me know!

- You are such a great teacher/salesman/editor/etc. I know it's hard to have to look for a new position, but I have great faith in your abilities. May God find you just the right place in the near future.

- It was a shock to learn you have been laid off. It's simply not right and not fair. Remember that your friends are here for you and will be praying you'll know God's grace and peace during this difficult time.

The End of a Relationship

- One of the most difficult things in life is coming to realize that the person you are totally in love with isn't the right one for you long term. May the Lord heal your heart.

- I am sorry. Trust that God is in control and will heal your broken heart. You two are both great people, and God will lead you each to the person who is right for you.

- I'll be praying for you, my friend. I'm so sorry you're hurting. That pain is all too familiar to me and I don't wish it for people I love.

- Thinking of you and praying for you. I know it has got to be heartbreaking even though you know it is the right thing.

- You are so precious. I cannot fathom the depth of your despair. Please know that you are in my prayers and on my heart. I love you, dear friend.

- I'm so sorry. I know God will heal your heart, but I'm sure it doesn't feel like it right now.

- I wanted to let you know that I'm praying God will comfort you with the comfort only He can give.

General Disappointments and Struggles

- This has been such a difficult season for you! I'm praying that it is a season that soon will have run its course, and that things will take a turn for the better very soon.

- You are such a wonderful person and friend; it isn't fair that you've gone through so much lately. I want to assure you that I care and want to do whatever I can to help. I've been praying, but will talk to you soon about other ways to help during these difficult days.

- Remember when we were a lot younger and life was simple? I miss those times. But we do still have each other and a future of good things to anticipate. Hang in there and remember you are loved.

- I know you are disappointed about what has happened. Just remember, I'll never be disappointed in you!

Depression

- We share so much in common, including struggles like those you are going through right now. Let me know if talking will help. I'm here for you, praying and wanting to help.

- While I can't possibly know what it's like for you right now, I'm hurting for you. May God be with you in your difficult times and give you the hope of a brighter day to come.

- You are such an important part of my world. Thank you for bringing so much to our friendship. I'm sorry to learn that you are having a very tough time, and want to let you know I care.

Loss of a Dream

- What a painful loss for you! I hope you know that I understand how much this (dream) means to you and how hard it is to see it slip away. I am praying for you and hoping for better days ahead.
- When a dream dies, part of us dies too. But you have so much to offer this world. I admire and respect all you give to this life, and anticipate the times we will have to talk and share in the future. May God put His arms around you during this hard time.
- Your loss of this dream is very, very tough. I know it must feel like it's hard to go on in the face of it. But please know that I am here for you and want to walk through this time with you.

Aunt Me-me's Guide to What *Not* to Say

Let me state again, Aunt Me-me means well. She really does. But she likes to shoot from the hip and all too often dashes off that note or email without ever rereading it to see how it comes across. A whirlwind of action is Me-me, but whirlwinds can stir things up and leave damage in their wake.

These are some examples from Aunt Me-me's infamous collection of off-track cards and letters:

- Lost your job? Don't think of it as unemployment. Think of it as an extended vacation. (I envy you and sure wish I had that kind of time on my hands these days.) Since you'll have lots of free time, maybe you'd like to drop by and help with the garden. Just remember I don't have any money to pay you. That's what unemployment compensation is for, right?

- So you broke up with Lose-y McLoserson. You must believe it's God's will. That guy would never have made you happy. He didn't deserve you! And even if he was the dumper, and you were the dumpee, it's a blessing in disguise! So pick yourself up, put on your makeup, and start looking again. There's a lot of fish in the sea, right, sister?

- Hey, I wanted to drop you a line since I never see you anymore. We used to have such fun. Now you don't answer my calls and you never write. Did you know you missed my birthday? I heard from Thelma that you're having a little bout of "the blues." Honey, I've been singing that tune my whole life. But do I make a big deal about it? No, I pick myself up and dust myself off. Get off your duff and onto your knees and start praying; you'll be feeling better in no time. And call me! We can do lunch. I'd hate to lose our friendship just because you're down in the dumps. But it's a two-way street, isn't it? Seriously, call me.

Among Me-me's worst traits is that of minimizing other people's feelings and situations. She can't stand to feel bad, so she tells everybody else they shouldn't feel bad.

She makes judgments based on very little information and then launches into her lecture from there. Of course, she throws in some "spiritual advice," knowing that you can't argue with God (or with her when she thinks she's speaking for Him). Me-me also tends to insert herself into every problem, because no matter what you are suffering, she's had it worse!

Me-me also puts the pressure on her hurting friend to do things for her! After laying on the guilt, preaching a little sermon, and complaining about her own life, she leaves it up to her friend to take action.

Most of us aren't as obvious in our missteps, but when you write that note, letter, or Facebook comment, ask yourself first which party you're truly trying to comfort in the situation. If you're trying to ease your personal pain at the expense of your friend, you need to stop, pray, and rephrase your communication.

What Others Say: Quotes Worth Sharing

Words of comfort, skillfully administered, are the oldest therapy known to man.

Louis Nizer

Although the world is full of suffering, it is full also of the overcoming of it.

Helen Keller

When things are bad, we take comfort in the thought that they could always be worse. And when they are, we find hope in the thought that things are so bad, they have to get better.

Malcolm S. Forbes, *The Sayings of Chairman Malcolm*

Storms make trees take deeper roots.

Claude McDonald, *The Christian Word*

It is the wounded oyster that mends its shell with pearl.

Ralph Waldo Emerson

Start by doing what is necessary, then what is possible, and suddenly you are doing the impossible.

St. Francis of Assisi

Measure wealth not by the things you have, but by the things you have for which you would not take money.

Anonymous

Scripture Passages to Read or Quote

Finally, brothers and sisters, rejoice! Strive for full restoration, encourage one another, be of one mind, live in peace. And the God of love and peace will be with you.

2 Corinthians 13:11

You, LORD, hear the desire of the afflicted; you encourage them, and you listen to their cry.

Psalm 10:17

Consider how the wild flowers grow. They do not labor or spin. Yet I tell you, not even Solomon in all his splendor was dressed like one of these. If that is how God clothes the grass of the field, which is here today, and tomorrow is thrown into the fire, how much more will he clothe you.

Luke 12:27–28

For everything that was written in the past was written to teach us, so that through the endurance taught in the Scriptures and the encouragement they provide we might have hope. May the God who gives endurance and encouragement give you the same attitude of mind toward each other that Christ Jesus had, so that with one mind and one voice you may glorify the God and Father of our Lord Jesus Christ.

Romans 15:4–6

So then, brothers and sisters, stand firm and hold fast to the teachings we passed on to you, whether by word of mouth or by letter. May our Lord Jesus Christ himself and God our Father, who loved us and by his grace gave us eternal encouragement and good hope, encourage your hearts and strengthen you in every good deed and word.

2 Thessalonians 2:15–17

"For I know the plans I have for you," declares the Lord, "plans to prosper you and not to harm you, plans to give you hope and a future."

Jeremiah 29:11

Come to me, all you who are weary and burdened, and I will give you rest. Take my yoke upon you and learn from me, for I am gentle and humble in heart, and you will find rest for your souls. For my yoke is easy and my burden is light.

Matthew 11:28–30

Do not be anxious about anything, but in every situation, by prayer and petition, with thanksgiving, present your requests to God. And the peace of God, which transcends all understanding, will guard your hearts and your minds in Christ Jesus.

Philippians 4:6–7

The Lord is with me; I will not be afraid. What can mere mortals do to me?

Psalm 118:6

Be strong and courageous. Do not be afraid or terrified because of them, for the Lord your God goes with you; he will never leave you nor forsake you.

Deuteronomy 31:6

What, then, shall we say in response to these things? If God is for us, who can be against us? He who did not spare his own Son, but gave him up for us all—how will he not also, along with him, graciously give us all things?

Romans 8:31–32

Grace and peace be yours in abundance.

1 Peter 1:2

Where can I go from your Spirit?
   Where can I flee from your presence?
If I go up to the heavens, you are there;
   if I make my bed in the depths, you are there.
If I rise on the wings of the dawn,
   if I settle on the far side of the sea,
even there your hand will guide me,
   your right hand will hold me fast.

Psalm 139:7–10

the person or people who will be receiving your message. Write down "feeling" words too.

- Think about a similar event in your own life. Did you receive any special words of congratulations that meant a lot to you? What were they?

- Read through the Scripture passages in this chapter and let them inspire you to share words that will uplift and encourage others.

Words to Make Your Own

Birth and Adoption

- We were thrilled to get your good news about the arrival of [baby's name]. What fun it will be to share your joy when we meet her in person. For now we rejoice from a distance!

- I am so looking forward to meeting little [baby's name]. May God bless you as you welcome this precious child into your family.

- What a blessing to hear of this new life welcomed into the world. I trust God will grant you every joy as you celebrate his arrival.

- Your family has grown! We are so excited for you and want to help in any way possible. Please know we are praying for you during this time of adjustment and transition.

- You have a special new family member, and we want to celebrate with you! We praise God for bringing this much-anticipated change into your lives.

Graduation

- Congratulations on your high school graduation! You've worked hard for this day, and we are so proud of you.
- May God bless you as you march into a bright future.
- We have been praying for you throughout your school years and rejoice with you as you mark your graduation day.
- We've known you ever since you were a baby, so it seems hard to believe you have just graduated from college. You've made your family proud and we have been privileged to watch you grow into a fine young woman/man.
- I continue to pray that God's hand of blessing will be on you as you move into a new season of life. Congratulations!
- May you feel a terrific sense of accomplishment in all you have achieved with God's help. You've worked hard for this!
- What an accomplishment to go back to school and get your degree! May the Lord guide you into this next, exciting phase of your life.

Promotion

- I was so happy to hear of your promotion! May your new position meet all your expectations and lead you further to fulfilling your dreams.
- You are so deserving of the new job. Congratulations on being the right person at the right time. I know you will do great!
- What great news about your promotion. May God bless you as you tackle the learning curve and make your mark in your new position!

- I'm thrilled about your good news! And I continue to pray that God will equip you to do your very best throughout your career and all the changes it brings.
- You worked so hard and now you've earned a promotion. I am proud of you and know you'll make the best of it in every way. Congratulations!

Retirement

- The day has finally arrived. I wish you all the very best on your retirement and in all the exciting days to come.
- May God bless you as you retire and move into the next season He has planned for your life.
- You have been such an outstanding leader and example of a godly worker. May you enjoy the rewards and challenges of retirement as you set about a new and different field of ministry.
- Retirement is a time of transition, filled with expectation and exciting changes. I pray the Lord will bless you during these days and surround you with people to enjoy them with too!

Aunt Me-me's Guide to What *Not* to Say

It's hard to go too far astray when offering words related to celebrations and congratulations. Still, if anybody can step on the one mine in a field of flowers, it's Aunt Me-me.

Her biggest problem is it's always about Me-me. She just can't get the spotlight off herself and focus on others. At the same time, if she feels any twinge of anxiety or concern about a situation, those negative feelings often end up in her writing. Here are some good (bad) examples:

- I'm so glad to hear you've given me another niece to love! I can't wait until she's old enough to really get to know me.

- Wow, twins! I can't imagine how you're going to afford your growing family, but I'm sure you'll figure it out somehow!

- I'm happy to hear you adopted a baby. I know she'll be a great addition and fit in well with your natural children.

- Congratulations on your adoption. Of course, now you'll probably get pregnant! Isn't that what always happens? The more the merrier, I'm sure.

- So you've graduated! Good luck getting a job in this tough economy. I'm sure you'll beat the odds, though. You've got the family genes for getting by on very little money.

- Congratulations! You've been in college for so long, I almost forgot you were there. Now, make your parents proud and start paying off those huge loans. I'm rooting for you!

- I heard about your promotion. Congratulations! Now that you're making more money, I expect you can start paying for lunch when we go out. You can write off all my good advice as "consulting"!

- How brave of you to retire in such uncertain times. In my family, people worked until they dropped. Enjoy your years of leisure. Feel free to drop by and weed my garden for me!

- I wanted to congratulate you on your retirement. Maybe someday when I get to retire we can get together for a picnic or something. I guess you can see I'm a little jealous, bless your heart!

Aunt Me-me's passive aggression isn't very thinly disguised, is it? Sure, most of us are sensitive enough not to make such blatant mistakes, but we can go down that road in more subtle ways.

Be sure to reread what you write to make sure you can't be misinterpreted or haven't let ideas slip through that could be hurtful. For example, don't bring up negatives or let fear color a message that should otherwise be uplifting and helpful. Celebration is a time for focusing on the brightest aspects of life.

What Others Say: Quotes Worth Sharing

Birth and Adoption

We never know the love of the parent till we become parents ourselves.

Henry Ward Beecher

Making the decision to have a child—it's momentous. It is to decide forever to have your heart go walking around outside your body.

Elizabeth Stone

Grandchildren are God's way of compensating us for growing old.

Mary H. Waldrip

Children are the living messages we send to a time we will not see.

John W. Whitehead, *The Stealing of America*

111

Graduation

The quality of a man's life is in direct proportion to his commitment to excellence, regardless of his chosen field of endeavor.

Vince Lombardi

Never give in . . . in nothing, great or small, large or petty— never give in except to convictions of honor and good sense.

Winston Churchill

The world is before you, and you need not take it or leave it as it was when you came in.

James Baldwin

I make the most of all that comes and the least of all that goes.

Sara Teasdale

Promotion

Never let the fear of striking out get in your way.

Babe Ruth

The reward for work well done is the opportunity to do more.

Jonas Salk, MD

When we do the best we can, we never know what miracle is wrought in our life, or in the life of another.

Helen Keller

Retirement

Retirement should be based on the tread, not the mileage.

Allen Ludden

Work consists of whatever a body is obliged to do, and play consists of whatever a body is not obliged to do.

Mark Twain, *The Adventures of Tom Sawyer*

If life were just, we would be born old and achieve youth about the time we'd saved enough to enjoy it.

Jim Fiebig

Scripture Passages to Read or Quote

Birth and Adoption

Let the heavens rejoice, let the earth be glad; let them say among the nations, "The LORD reigns!"

1 Chronicles 16:31

Our mouths were filled with laughter,
    our tongues with songs of joy.
Then it was said among the nations,
    "The LORD has done great things for them."
The LORD has done great things for us,
    and we are filled with joy.

Psalm 126:2–3

For you created my inmost being;
    you knit me together in my mother's womb.
I praise you because I am fearfully and wonderfully
    made;
    your works are wonderful,
    I know that full well.

Psalm 139:13–14

Graduation

Wisdom, like an inheritance, is a good thing
and benefits those who see the sun.
Wisdom is a shelter
as money is a shelter,
but the advantage of knowledge is this:
Wisdom preserves those who have it.

Ecclesiastes 7:11–12

The quiet words of the wise are more to be heeded than the shouts of a ruler of fools.

Ecclesiastes 9:17

Whatever you do, work at it with all your heart, as working for the Lord, not for human masters.

Colossians 3:23

Promotion

Sovereign LORD, you have begun to show to your servant your greatness and your strong hand. For what god is there in heaven or on earth who can do the deeds and mighty works you do?

Deuteronomy 3:24

Shout for joy to the LORD, all the earth.
Worship the LORD with gladness;
come before him with joyful songs.
For the LORD is good and his love endures forever;
his faithfulness continues through all
generations.

Psalm 100:1–2, 5

Retirement

Since my youth, God, you have taught me,
    and to this day I declare your marvelous deeds.
Even when I am old and gray,
    do not forsake me, my God,
till I declare your power to the next generation,
    your mighty acts to all who are to come.
Your righteousness, God, reaches to the heavens,
    you who have done great things.
Who is like you, God?

Psalm 71:17–19

The LORD bless you
    and keep you;
the LORD make his face shine on you
    and be gracious to you;
the LORD turn his face toward you
    and give you peace.

Numbers 6:24–26

Now finish the work, so that your eager willingness to do
it may be matched by your completion of it, according to
your means.

2 Corinthians 8:11

We remember before our God and Father your work produced
by faith, your labor prompted by love, and your endurance
inspired by hope in our Lord Jesus Christ.

1 Thessalonians 1:3

8

Words for Events and Activities

Beyond the special events already covered in this book, life provides many other occasions for invitations and acceptances: birthday parties, baby showers, significant wedding anniversaries, retirement celebrations, work-related events, fund-raisers, and much more. This chapter will focus on both gracious invitations and grateful responses.

These occasions may also prompt special messages of affirmation and appreciation, oftentimes accompanied by a gift. Those messages (not to mention the gifts!) are gratefully received, even if the messages of appreciation arrive for no special reason at all. So we'll explore how you can send grace-filled words in those cases.

And finally, as believers, we often include our close friends and family members in our requests for prayer. Regular prayer requests are shared in Bible study groups and in other small-group settings, sometimes for many months and even years. It's important to thank people for their prayers and share the outcome with them when those prayers are answered.

Words of Invitation

More and more often, people are using online invitations such as evite or Facebook events to ask friends and family to join them in activities. There is nothing wrong with these approaches, especially if your circle includes mostly Internet-savvy folks who regularly use electronic communications. If you're sending out invitations to people you aren't sure own iPhones or use computers (e.g., invitations to your parents' friends for a fiftieth wedding anniversary), first consider your recipients as you choose your invitation format.

Match the invitation to the occasion and decide how formal or informal you want to go. Your occasion could fall into one of many categories, from one-of-a-kind celebrations to something ongoing such as participating in a book club. Here are some guidelines to keep in mind:

- Be clear about the type of occasion (baby shower, birthday party, fund-raiser, etc.), and state it first: Please join us for a 50th birthday party for Kathy, Lisa, and Liz; You're invited to a special fund-raiser to help schoolchildren in Togo; It's an open house! Come see our new offices.
- Give details in an easy-to-scan style: date (including day of week) and time.
- Include the location, address, a map, and driving directions.

- Will there be refreshments? If so, specify. (E.g., light refreshments will be served; tea and cookies will be provided; lunch will be served, etc.).

- Provide instructions for a response: RSVP; Please respond; or Regrets only. Include a phone number, email address, or reply card and addressed envelope for more formal invitations. Include a date by which you need the response. (Please respond by [date].)

- If appropriate, add information about dress (black tie, formal, casual, in costume), such as: Casual dress is suggested.

- If your event is planned for the outdoors, you may want to include an alternate date or place in case of rain.

- Be sure it's clear who is issuing the invitation. You can say something like: [Name] requests the pleasure of your company . . . The invitation is issued in the names of all those hosting the event. The invitee should respond using that name(s).

- If you want to specify "no gifts," a gracious way of doing that is: "Your friendship is a special gift; we respectfully request no other." Or ask for a contribution to a memory book or advice cards to honor the guest(s).

- If you don't hear back from invitees, you will have to contact them and ask if they will be attending.

Words of Acceptance

A person finds joy in giving an apt reply—and how good is a timely word!

Proverbs 15:23

The key to a gracious acceptance lies more in the timing than in choosing the right words. Don't delay; accept today! Why would you postpone such a happy task anyway? When you take too long to accept, it could send the message that you were just waiting for a better offer to come along. So here is a list of do's for accepting offers and invitations.

- Answer promptly.
- If your acceptance is late, you can apologize, but don't dwell on it or offer excuses.
- Be sure your "yes" is loud and clear.
- Be excited. Add a sentence that tells why you are so happy to accept the invitation or offer.
- Express your thanks.
- If there is any possibility of misunderstanding, be sure to confirm the details of what you are saying yes to.
- If you have to cancel after accepting an invitation, call the person or host right away, then send a follow-up note apologizing for having to change plans. You may even want to send flowers with your note if your cancellation created an inconvenience of any kind.

Words of Appreciation and Affirmation

Have you ever received an unexpected note or letter from a friend or family member who just wanted to tell you how wonderful you are? If so, you understand how amazingly affirming those words can be in your life. Words have the power to shape the way we feel about ourselves and can give us the motivation to go out and do great things!

As I mentioned in the Introduction, I work at Compassion International, where a major aspect of our ministry to children in poverty includes sponsors who write letters to their sponsored children. These kids desperately need to hear how much they matter to their sponsors, and know they are special in God's eyes, so they can find hope for the future. One young woman named Michelle, a graduate of the program who went on to earn a master's degree, says that during her childhood, family members told her she was ugly because she resembled her father, who abandoned the family. Only her sponsor told her she was beautiful. She clung to those positive words as she grew into a woman who fulfilled her God-given potential.

Who can you encourage and affirm today? Perhaps your message of appreciation will accompany a gift to celebrate a graduation, anniversary, or birthday. Or maybe you'll take time to speak into someone's life today and just let that person know how important he or she is to you and why. Here are some examples:

- May God bless you today and every day. I'm so thankful He sent you into my life to be my friend and encourager.
- Thank you for standing with me through good times and bad times. Without your prayers, help, and laughter, I'm not sure I'd be where I am today.
- What an outstanding person you have grown up to be. I admire the way you reach out to help others and take time for the really important things in life.
- Thank you for being an example of faith in action.
- When I first met you, I had no idea what good friends we would become. How grateful I am for your wisdom and

excellent advice. We've shared so many cups of coffee, there's no way to count them. Each one represents time together that has built me up as a person and changed my life for the better. Thank you.

• You have been a great role model for me. Thank you for your sacrifice of time and energy to help me become the person I am today. May God bless you richly!

Words About Answers to Prayer

Many of us belong to a group that prays together on a regular basis. We share our deepest concerns, most heartfelt needs, and greatest hopes and dreams. We may also share our prayer requests with friends and relatives we know will be faithful to uphold us in prayer. When answers to our prayers come, it's a wonderful time to tell or write to our fellow believers as a way of thanking them and encouraging them in their own faith.

I really do believe in the old adage that there are three possible answers to prayer: yes, no, and wait. When the answer is yes, we celebrate. When it's no, we grieve. And when it's wait, well, what do we do? For instance, a couple going through infertility can experience years of waiting before the answer to their prayer for a baby is a definitive yes or no. How do you bring close friends and family along on your journey as they accompany you in prayer? At some point, a thoughtful written message may help you express your feelings about the situation.

When you have received a positive resolution to a prayer request, do share it in celebration with those who prayed for you and with you. Here are a few possible expressions of joy:

- Thank you so much for praying for a job for Jacob. We are so grateful that he has found the right job at last, and that you have traveled this road by our sides all these many months. We praise God for His provision!

- You have been so faithful in praying for us to add to our family. Now that a new baby is on the way, we want to thank you for being there for us, both in the past and in the exciting days to come.

- I'm so glad you are part of my life! Thank you for sharing in all the ups and downs and trials and tribulations of my search for a spouse. As the wedding day approaches, I want to let you know how much I thank God for you and all your friendship means to me. He has answered my prayer and also given me a faithful friend in you. I'm so grateful.

What about prayers that have been fervently offered—whether for healing, to save a marriage, to adopt a child, or anything desperately desired—that didn't happen as hoped for? When the answer is no, it's important to remember that God isn't a cosmic genie who exists to grant our wishes. He is God and we worship Him in all circumstances. Some messages could include the following:

- I want you to know how much I treasure the times we spent in prayer together. Though the answer wasn't what we hoped for, we can rest assured that God's love will provide promised comfort in the midst of this loss. Thank you so much for praying faithfully in these past months.

- Your love, care, and prayers have meant so much during these difficult times. Please know that even with a disappointing outcome, the time we shared on our knees together is a memory I will always hold deeply.

- Because of your faithful prayers, I continue to experience the love of God even in this time of loss. I know you care and I know you will continue to pray for my recovery and God's restoration.

When the answer to a prayer request is to wait, it can be wise to hold on to the truth about God as stated in Scripture. Messages could include the following reminders and Scripture verses:

- Thank you for holding firm in prayer for me, though the answer has been so slow in coming. Remember, "The LORD is my strength and my defense; he has become my salvation. He is my God, and I will praise him, my father's God, and I will exalt him" (Exodus 15:2).
- I believe that eventually, we will have an answer to the prayers we have been praying so long. Together let's lean on this promise: "Taste and see that the LORD is good; blessed is the one who takes refuge in him" (Psalm 34:8).
- It has been a great comfort to know you have been praying and will continue to pray. It does make a difference in how I get through each day. "Surely God is my help; the Lord is the one who sustains me" (Psalm 54:4).
- Thank you for continuing to pray for me during these difficult times. Let us be reminded of this promise from His Word: "The Lord is faithful, and he will strengthen you and protect you from the evil one" (2 Thessalonians 3:3).

Aunt Me-me's Guide to What *Not* to Say

This chapter's guide to avoiding trouble will focus on promotional parties. You know what I mean—those regular invitations to social occasions organized around sales and buying opportunities, giving you the chance to mingle with friends while sampling, handling, and purchasing tasty dips and food mixes, cooking supplies, makeup, candles, jewelry, and handbags.

Like many of us, outgoing Aunt Me-me loves these little get-togethers. She enjoys the variety, buying gifts for herself and others, and the way these parties bring her together with friends both old and new. She's been a buyer and a hostess, enthusiastic about trying it all.

But Me-me—in her single-mindedness—is running into some problems with this model of socializing.

First, her dedication to finding some kind of business that works for her is leading her to burn out her small circle of friends and family because she just plans too many parties for the same group of people.

Second, her own commitment to attending everybody else's events is breaking her budget and eating up all her "fun money." What's the answer?

What *not* to do is the path poor Me-me usually chooses:

- She pressures her "peeps" to come because she really needs the money.
- She plans ever more and different events, and lays on the guilt so people will keep attending.
- She pesters her friends about whether or not they are going to be there.

- She stalks their Facebook pages to see if they really have other plans, then confronts them if it looks like they don't.
- She makes up excuses when she doesn't want to go to someone else's party. None of them sound very plausible.
- She's even invented a whole other life via social media to "prove" she really couldn't be there.

In reality, handling these parties with tact and grace is a simple matter. If you don't want to go, don't go. Just tell the truth that you don't enjoy them, or that you have no plans to ever host them yourself. If it's truly a budget matter, that's up to you to disclose. You aren't required to say you're on a tight budget and have nothing extra to spend. But you're also not required to use a lame excuse as a way of getting out of the activity.

Do remember that the event is still a social event, and the person hosting the party would no doubt appreciate your attendance, even if you have no plans to buy. I suggest you simply make it clear when you accept the invitation. You can promise to look at, sample, and even enthuse about the merchandise, even if you aren't planning to bring a credit card, debit card, or checkbook. The party will be more fun because you are there, and you won't feel any pressure to purchase merchandise you don't want or can't afford.

Whatever you do, don't ignore the invitation. RSVP generally means you should respond with a yes or a no and do so as quickly as possible.

And creating fiction on your Facebook or other social media accounts is never advised, no matter how much you want to invent an alternate life to get out of uncomfortable situations. Speak the truth. And do it lovingly.

What Others Say: Quotes Worth Sharing

If a window of opportunity appears, don't pull down the shade.

Tom Peters, The Pursuit of Wow!

When you have to make a choice, and don't make it, that is in itself a choice.

William James

Half our life is spent trying to find something to do with the time we have rushed through life trying to save.

Will Rogers

The Present is the point at which time touches eternity.

C. S. Lewis, The Screwtape Letters

Life is not dated merely by years. Events are sometimes the best calendars.

Benjamin Disraeli

There is no love sincerer than the love of food.

George Bernard Shaw

Never eat more than you can lift.

Miss Piggy's Guide to Life, as told to Henry Beard

Scripture Passages to Read or Quote

Let my teaching fall like rain
and my words descend like dew,
like showers on new grass,
like abundant rain on tender plants.

I will proclaim the name of the LORD.
  Oh, praise the greatness of our God!
He is the Rock, his works are perfect,
  and all his ways are just.
A faithful God who does no wrong,
  upright and just is he.

Deuteronomy 32:2–4

The trumpeters and musicians joined in unison to give praise and thanks to the LORD. Accompanied by trumpets, cymbals and other instruments, the singers raised their voices in praise to the LORD and sang: "He is good; his love endures forever."

2 Chronicles 5:13

So we fasted and petitioned our God about this, and he answered our prayer.

Ezra 8:23

Many, LORD, are asking, "Who will bring us
  prosperity?"
  Let the light of your face shine on us.
Fill my heart with joy
  when their grain and new wine abound.

Psalm 4:6–7

I call on you, my God, for you will answer me;
  turn your ear to me and hear my prayer.

Psalm 17:6

Praise be to the LORD,
  for he has heard my cry for mercy.
The LORD is my strength and my shield;
  my heart trusts in him, and he helps me.

My heart leaps for joy,
   and with my song I praise him.

                       Psalm 28:6–7

Praise be to the LORD,
   for he showed me the wonders of his love
   when I was in a city under siege.

                       Psalm 31:21

Is anyone among you in trouble? Let them pray. Is anyone happy? Let them sing songs of praise.

                       James 5:13

9

Words of Truth and Love

Some messages are harder to deliver than others: confessing you've hurt another person and asking for forgiveness, for example, or granting forgiveness when you've been deeply hurt. It can be extremely difficult to confront someone you care about with a hard truth. It's even a struggle sometimes to open up and ask for prayer. We may fear that level of transparency or vulnerability.

While some of these difficult messages will naturally be conveyed in a conversation, one way to open the door is by writing a heartfelt message or letter detailing your thoughts and feelings. Putting the message in writing allows you to take time with your expression, explore the honest truth, and get your message across clearly yet with compassion.

This kind of communication is a sign of maturity, as we read in Ephesians 4:14–15: "Then we will no longer be infants, tossed back and forth by the waves, and blown here and there by every wind of teaching and by the cunning and craftiness of people in their deceitful scheming. Instead, speaking the truth in love, we will grow to become in every respect the mature body of him who is the head, that is, Christ."

Speaking truth, tempered with love, comes easily to some, but it is a skill to be developed by others. The key to the process is sincerity and humility.

Guidelines for Finding the Right Words

Let's start by exploring forgiveness. So often in our contemporary culture, this process has been simplified to offering an apology. But giving and receiving forgiveness is much more than a simple "I'm sorry" answered by an "I forgive you." Forgiveness is an example set by Jesus Christ himself: "Bear with each other and forgive one another if any of you has a grievance against someone. Forgive as the Lord forgave you" (Colossians 3:13).

Here are some steps for getting started on the road to asking for forgiveness:

- Think about what happened and what it is you are sorry for doing.
- Write out an apology that states clearly what it is you are sorry for.
- Acknowledge your actions without making excuses.
- Share your feelings about what happened. Avoid blaming, exaggerating, or writing empty words.
- Offer to make amends if appropriate.

Accepting an apology and granting forgiveness can be extremely difficult, especially when the hurt was intentional.

Even when the offense was caused by carelessness or neglect, it can be tough to fight feelings of anger and overcome that temptation to refuse to forgive. But we are instructed to overcome our natural reactions when we have been hurt this way. Jesus spoke very clearly on the subject in the Sermon on the Mount:

> You have heard that it was said to the people long ago, "You shall not murder, and anyone who murders will be subject to judgment." But I tell you that anyone who is angry with a brother or sister will be subject to judgment. Again, anyone who says to a brother or sister, "Raca," is answerable to the court. And anyone who says, "You fool!" will be in danger of the fire of hell.
>
> Therefore, if you are offering your gift at the altar and there remember that your brother or sister has something against you, leave your gift there in front of the altar. First go and be reconciled to them; then come and offer your gift.
>
> Matthew 5:21–24

Words to Make Your Own

Apology and Asking for Forgiveness

- I offended you when I made that negative remark about you, especially in front of others. Please forgive me.
- I know I hurt your feelings last night with the things I said about the dinner. I am truly sorry. Please forgive me.
- I am deeply sorry for blaming you for our project's outcome. I hope you will forgive me and that we can move forward from here.

133

- Please forgive me for missing a second lunch date in a row. I have no excuse, other than my own disorganization. I hope you'll give me one more chance and let me treat you to lunch next week.

Granting Forgiveness

- I appreciate your apology and want you to know I forgive you.
- While it has been a struggle, I want to extend grace and forgiveness to you as the Lord has encouraged us to. "Finally, brothers and sisters, rejoice! Strive for full restoration, encourage one another, be of one mind, live in peace. And the God of love and peace will be with you" (2 Corinthians 13:11).
- I know it was difficult for you to ask for forgiveness after what happened. Please be assured that I have forgiven you and want to put this in the past.
- As a fellow believer, I am thankful we have this direction from Jesus to help us know how to move forward: "Do not judge, and you will not be judged. Do not condemn, and you will not be condemned. Forgive, and you will be forgiven" (Luke 6:37). I do forgive you.

Words of Confrontation

What should you do when people close to you are behaving in ways that are hurtful and that go against biblical principles and God's directives? How can you "speak the truth in love" without being seen as interfering or fulfilling your own agenda? This is a tough question, one often faced by parents of grown children who are hurting themselves or others by their choices and actions.

When your children are fighting with each other, or your siblings are having a family dispute, or your relatives want you to agree with something that goes against your convictions, how do you respond while keeping the lines of communication open? The most effective approach involves being honest and compassionate at the same time. "Finally, all of you, be like-minded, be sympathetic, love one another, be compassionate and humble" (1 Peter 3:8).

Not everyone will see things the way you do, but you can gently confront and be clear about your perspective. Remember to emphasize the positive aspects of your relationship, and be tactful when offering correction or constructive criticism. Well-chosen words written in a letter may have a better chance of being received thoughtfully than words spoken in anger in a face-to-face or phone conversation.

When the apostle Paul wrote to the Corinthians in order to correct behaviors that were damaging the church, he expressed his feelings about them in no uncertain terms: "For I wrote you out of great distress and anguish of heart and with many tears, not to grieve you but to let you know the depth of my love for you" (2 Corinthians 2:4). What a beautiful example of speaking the truth in love.

Read through the Scripture passages at the end of this chapter to find words to inspire your own expressions of truth and love in the midst of conflict. Or let the following examples prompt you to initiate a caring discussion. Do beware of unleashing your opinions and "helpful insights" in one long, written rant instead of a dialogue that better conveys your interest in the other person's point of view.

- God's Word tells us to be reconciled to each other (see Matthew 5:21–24). It's obvious that you and I have a problem between us that needs to be talked about. Let's make an effort to speak honestly very soon.

- Judging one another is not right, in the very words of Jesus (see Matthew 7). But I feel some judgments have been made on both our parts that have created a rift between us. I hope we can meet face to face to share at a deeper level and resolve the issues between us.

- While I care very much about our relationship, some things have come up recently that need to be discussed seriously. Because I care so much about God's Word and His direction in Scripture, I can't ignore what is happening in your life. Can we talk soon?

Words for Difficult Times

It can also be a real challenge to find the right words when we ourselves are going through a difficult experience: a serious illness, a divorce, a job loss, or other circumstance that affects the circle of people in our lives. You may want to write a general letter or email that explains the situation and helps people understand how you are coping with it. While it can be a struggle to capture the perfect words at these times, you may find it provides a special opportunity to share your faith, especially with people in your life who know you are a believer but don't understand what that really means.

For example, I was inspired when I received this email from a man facing serious heart surgery.

During vacation, as part of my annual physical, my doctors found significant blockage in the arteries of my heart. Monday I meet with a surgeon to schedule a heart bypass as soon as possible.

The path God has given me has come to some rough terrain. I do not know where the path leads. I have much I would love to continue to do in my ministry and with my family. I believe that is His will too. If not, I do not question the path; I only seek His gift of sure and steady feet.

I share this part of my journey with you for a couple of reasons. God has already answered my prayers for healing (I have the best medical team one could ask for) and for peace (I am sure the path is the one He wishes for me).

Please pray for my family. They carry the burden of worry for me as husband, dad, and grandpa. Pray God will teach them (through me) how to walk the tough parts of life's path, and that they will see the presence of God in every step.

Please pray for me. I have the peace of knowing I am in God's hands. Pray I will know God's promised presence every step. Pray that the surgeons would be His instruments and that He would be glorified whatever the path.

I also share this with you to encourage you in knowing that I still seek to walk as Jesus walked and this has only strengthened my resolve to do so. Do not be discouraged or dismayed. His path leads to life and blessing. And He will provide sure feet for you and for me.

The writer of this email was able to share his news and prayer requests in a way that expressed his faith and trust in the Lord. He used it to encourage as well as explain the situation. What a clear example of being truthful about a very scary situation, while loving those in his circle enough to honestly communicate his hopes and his expectations.

The following examples and Scripture passages may help prompt your own words when you need to ask for prayer or express your faith during difficult times of your own.

- Due to the nature of this illness, we are entering a season of many unknowns. Please remember to pray for our whole family as we take it one step at a time.

- We are so thankful for your friendship, especially in the midst of crisis and uncertainty. We trust you will pray for us, as well as stay in touch, no matter what the future brings.

- "I have learned to be content whatever the circumstances. I know what it is to be in need, and I know what it is to have plenty. I have learned the secret of being content in any and every situation, whether well fed or hungry, whether living in plenty or in want. I can do all this through him who gives me strength" (Philippians 4:11–13).

- I am leaning on the arms of the Lord during this time of struggle, and I hope you will do the same. "I will say of the LORD, 'He is my refuge and my fortress, my God, in whom I trust' " (Psalm 91:2).

- As we walk down this difficult road, we take comfort in the promises of God. "The LORD is good, a refuge in times of trouble. He cares for those who trust in him" (Nahum 1:7).

Aunt Me-me's Guide to What *Not* to Say

Asking for forgiveness is not one of Me-me's better talents. She tends to think she's never the one at fault, but will break down and apologize if she believes that's the only way to restore a relationship. Still, she really can't help handing out blame instead of just admitting she was wrong and asking for forgiveness.

Here are some examples *not* to follow:

- Please forgive me for whatever I did to offend you. I can't say I actually remember doing something wrong, but I'm sure if you feel bad about it, you must know.
- I'll forgive you if you forgive me. I think we were both equally in the wrong, and it doesn't seem fair for me to do all the forgiving in this case.
- You misunderstood me. I never meant for you to be offended by my choice of words. In fact, I was actually trying to compliment you. That's what I get for trying to be nice. Anyway, I'm sorry.
- I never meant to hurt your feelings. I guess you are just a lot more sensitive about these things than I am. I hope you'll get over it soon.

Me-me struggles with the number-one rule about apologizing: it's not all about Me-me. Her lack of humility makes her apologies ring hollow and lack authenticity. Her real problem has nothing to do with words and everything to do with the attitude of her heart.

What Others Have Said: Quotes Worth Sharing

The more a man knows, the more he forgives.

Catherine the Great

Wisdom is the quality that keeps you from getting into situations where you need it.

Doug Larson

Forgiveness is a funny thing. It warms the heart and cools the sting.

William Arthur Ward

If you haven't any charity in your heart, you have the worst kind of heart trouble.

Bob Hope

When a deep injury is done us, we never recover until we forgive.

Alan Paton

Lord, where we are wrong, make us willing to change; where we are right, make us easy to live with.

Reverend Peter Marshall

The truth of the matter is that you always know the right thing to do. The hard part is doing it.

Gen. H. Norman Schwarzkopf

An apology is the superglue of life. It can repair just about anything.

Lynn Johnston

Sandwich every bit of criticism between two heavy layers of praise.

Mary Kay Ash, *Mary Kay on People Management*

Scripture Passages to Read or Quote

LORD Almighty, blessed is the one who trusts in you.

Psalm 84:12

They will have no fear of bad news; their hearts are steadfast, trusting in the LORD.

Psalm 112:7

Your kingdom is an everlasting kingdom, and your dominion endures through all generations. The LORD is trustworthy in all he promises and faithful in all he does.

Psalm 145:13

Trust in the LORD forever, for the LORD, the LORD himself, is the Rock eternal.

Isaiah 26:4

Blessed is the one who trusts in the LORD, whose confidence is in him.

Jeremiah 17:7

For if you forgive other people when they sin against you, your heavenly Father will also forgive you. But if you do not forgive others their sins, your Father will not forgive your sins.

Matthew 6:14–15

Do not judge, or you too will be judged. For in the same way you judge others, you will be judged, and with the measure you use, it will be measured to you.

Why do you look at the speck of sawdust in your brother's eye and pay no attention to the plank in your own eye? How can you say to your brother, "Let me take the speck out of your eye," when all the time there is a plank in your own eye? You hypocrite, first take the plank out of your own eye, and then you will see clearly to remove the speck from your brother's eye.

Matthew 7:1–5

And when you stand praying, if you hold anything against anyone, forgive them, so that your Father in heaven may forgive you your sins.

Mark 11:25

Let us then approach God's throne of grace with confidence, so that we may receive mercy and find grace to help us in our time of need.

Hebrews 4:16

10

Words for a Changing World

There's this place I know all too well. I keep visiting it every day, even though it contains some dark and scary places, places filled with people I should not even keep company with. But I keep visiting because it also has many warm and welcoming spots, places where everybody knows my name.

This world is cyberspace, a world so easily accessed by the Internet and that little screen on my laptop. It offers me company, insights, opinions, information, and all kinds of entertainment. (I mean, who doesn't love the hilarity of Lolcats.com?) But the Internet is also filled with deep tunnels and hidden traps where I suddenly find myself looking around and asking, "How did I get here? And which way is out?"

Finding the Right Words for Cyberspace

Our ever-changing Internet offers a wide range of places to share our thoughts, our words, our photos, our lives. It's a very public forum that deals with everything from life's most boring details to its most interesting highlights. It is filled with social media like Twitter and Facebook, blogs of every sort, invitations to review or comment on practically anything, and even sites where I can offer comfort, such as Caringbridge.org and online obituaries.

The world of the Internet is one that begs for light that believers can share, but we too often add to the darkness by posting before we think, by putting others down, adding to the tension, and missing opportunities to share Good News in a place that sometimes thrives on bad news.

If you spend a lot of time online, you know what I'm talking about. You've seen the debates about religion that spring from an innocent movie review. Or the horrible examples of cyber-bullying plastered on well-meaning sites like YouTube. You've clicked away in disgust.

If you only use the web to Google recipes and get map directions, then you may not see the possibilities for good and evil. But even benign sites like Facebook have been witness to slander, character-slaughter, and nasty debates between friends of friends who don't really know each other but disagree about politics or faith.

My hope is that we can gain perspective on the best ways to use Internet communication in the cause of Christ. It's still a new medium, and many mistakes have been made. But we can make an effort to end the wars of words that don't really win others over and often make Christians look bad in our efforts to be "right."

In a recent example, HuffingtonPost.com ran an article about an atheist who paid for a billboard misquoting Thomas Jefferson. Supposedly he said, "I do not find in Christianity one redeeming feature. It is founded on fables and mythology." Unfortunately, this atheist didn't employ a fact-checker. In fact, there is no evidence that Thomas Jefferson ever made such a statement. The article was followed by more than 150 comments that quickly degenerated into name-calling between believers and atheists and agnostics.

One writer, "Lacy May," found a graceful way to offer her opinion without deliberately insulting those who wouldn't agree with her:

> Sad to see such polarization here when we should all embrace our beliefs and respect others whether they believe the same way or not! I'm a Christian who believes (without doubt) that Christ lived to show us how to love ourselves and others and live in harmony on this planet. I love Christ Jesus, NOT religion. For those who believe he was a mythological character, I encourage you to read Lee Strobel's "A Case for Christ." (Strobel was an atheist and respected journalist who set out to debunk Jesus only to find historical evidence about his actual life; http://leestrobel.com.) For those turned off by zealots who believe Christianity means you must insist that others believe and worship exactly as they do, check out, "When BAD Christians Happen to GOOD People," by Dave Burchett.
> Peace, Love, Healing & Hope to ALL[6]

I like how this writer is urging mutual respect while at the same time making a case for her faith. She includes links to helpful resources that may shed light on the topic, and wishes readers well. This doesn't mean comments that followed didn't attack her position, but her argument was respectful and reasonable. Such a response is a positive light, much needed in the wild-west-world of online comments.

If you're a person who likes to be part of the public forum, who can't resist commenting here, there, and everywhere, just remember to be sensitive. Not everybody on your friend's Facebook page thinks the same way you do. Not all Christians will cheer your staunch defense of Republicans or Glenn Beck in the name of Jesus. And not everybody applauds your fighting words.

Rational, level-headed, and compassionate commentary and discussion is a credit to the written word. But it's important to be wise and sensitive to your audience. And be especially careful about "speaking for God." You can quote Scripture and speak truth in a way that respects the opposite viewpoint. You can even respectfully disagree with fellow believers in a way that keeps us from looking like a bunch of infighting hypocrites. But that may mean rereading what you wrote before hitting the Submit button. Or even praying about it first!

Prompts to Help You Begin

Before you launch into a rant on your blog, comment on that ridiculous opinion piece, or straighten out a wrong-headed friend on Facebook, you may want to consider these Scripture passages and think about how to conform your words to the descriptions that follow:

- "We have different gifts, according to the grace given to each of us. If your gift is prophesying, then prophesy in accordance with your faith; if it is serving, then serve; if it is teaching, then teach; if it is to encourage, then give encouragement; if it is giving, then give generously; if it is to lead, do it diligently; if it is to show mercy, do it cheerfully" (Romans 12:6–8). What is your gift as a communicator?

- In what way have you been shown mercy by the Lord? "All of us also lived among them at one time, gratifying the cravings of our flesh and following its desires and thoughts. Like the rest, we were by nature deserving of wrath. But because of his great love for us, God, who is rich in mercy, made us alive with Christ even when we were dead in transgressions—it is by grace you have been saved" (Ephesians 2:3–5).

- "Love does not delight in evil but rejoices with the truth" (1 Corinthians 13:6). When you "speak the truth," do you do so in a spirit of love or a spirit of superiority?

- How humble are you when you post comments online? "I thank Christ Jesus our Lord, who has given me strength, that he considered me trustworthy, appointing me to his service. Even though I was once a blasphemer and a persecutor and a violent man, I was shown mercy because I acted in ignorance and unbelief. The grace of our Lord was poured out on me abundantly, along with the faith and love that are in Christ Jesus" (1 Timothy 1:12–14).

- "And the peace of God, which transcends all understanding, will guard your hearts and your minds in Christ Jesus. Finally, brothers and sisters, whatever is true, whatever is noble, whatever is right, whatever is pure, whatever is lovely, whatever is admirable—if anything is excellent or praiseworthy—think about such things. Whatever you have learned or received or heard from me, or seen in me—put it into practice. And the God of peace will be with you" (Philippians 4:7–9). Spend time evaluating your online life and presence. How well does it stack up to the standard described here?

- "But the wisdom that comes from heaven is first of all pure; then peace-loving, considerate, submissive, full of mercy and good fruit, impartial and sincere" (James 3:17). If this were a checklist of qualities for your own online postings, how many boxes would have a checkmark?

Words of Online Comfort

From time to time, different friends of mine who are experiencing extremely hard times have turned to a website called caringbridge.org. Whether struggling with a serious cancer diagnosis, a traumatic car accident, sudden loss of a spouse, or a loved one's battle with dementia, each has been able to give updates and receive comfort. It has become a beautiful place of community as people post their encouragement for all to see. So many posts are filled with hope and true statements about the love of the Lord.

This is the sort of communication that lifts my heart and helps me believe civilization isn't doomed after all. What a fantastic way to demonstrate real faith and caring to each other and the world at large. Here are some samples of postings on various sites' guest books. Use them as examples and inspiration when you have friends in similar situations.

- You, your family, and the medical staff are all in my continuing prayers and in the hands of the Great Physician. He is with all of you.

- Just a few moments ago I learned of your impending surgery. I am shocked. Please be assured of my prayers for you at this very stressful time. Peace!

- May God hold you close, give you comfort, guide your doctors and nurses, and bring you to full health and wholeness. Bless you, friend.

- Thanks for providing this place where we can uphold you in prayer. God is our refuge and strength. Praying for His watch and care over you.

- You don't know me, but I wanted you to know that I'm praying for you. God is a God of healing, deliverance, and miracles. With Him on your side, you've got everything you need.

- What a hard path you're on. There is no way for us to really know how hard. Our prayers and thoughts are with you.

- I was very happy to hear the results of the most recent treatment were favorable. May the recovery from this one be smooth and manageable.

- We were so thankful for the good news today and are continuing to remember all of you in our prayers. We especially pray for peace beyond your understanding and for wisdom from above for you and the doctors.

- We're in the darkest days of winter right now, but spring will come, just as the Lord will come back for those of us who remain and will join us together again with those that we love who have been invited home before us.

- I have been searching for the right words to express my sympathy for all you are going through. I finally realized there are never the right words. You have been an amazing example of unconditional love that has touched me more than you know. May God's grace and love uphold you and your family.

- We weep because the morning has not come yet, but JOY will be there when the Son rises. I'm sorry you are going through this. Our thoughts, prayers, and tears are with you all.

- May God continue to give you strength, peace, and comfort. I've been praying and thinking of you all, hoping that God will grant you peace in these last days.

- You have been on my mind and heart continuously these past few days. May God continue to give you strength and wisdom, and may many acts of love and kindness be evident to you as you experience God's faithfulness even during this difficult time.

- I'm so sorry to hear how things are going right now; I will continue to pray for you and all the family as the days go by. You remain in my heart. This morning especially I was reminded that God is always in control, no matter what we face. May He hold you up in every way!

- While we are present here on earth, in body and mind, the best thing we can do with our spirit is give it to one another, to express our love and concern, and to share whatever our strengths are with each other. I am thankful for the opportunity to be reminded that our greatest gift is to love one another.

- Our love goes out to all of you at this difficult time. I know God will direct and guide through the difficult decisions and times ahead. You are in and will continue to be in God's loving hands.

- I know we can be comforted by the message of Jesus, but it is still hard. We will be praying for God to sustain and strengthen you over the days to come.

- You and your extended family members have been in my prayers these past many weeks. I'll continue to pray as you shift your focus back home and help the kids adjust to this loss. Know that many people have been pulling for you in these sad days.

Aunt Me-me's Guide to What *Not* to Say

Aunt Me-me isn't much acquainted with the Internet, but she does love her Facebook interactions. Unfortunately, she often forgets there exists a means of private communications (it's called sending a message), and she ends up posting every thought in her head on her friends' Walls. This can result in unexpected problems when she doesn't stop to think.

- Thanks for posting that family portrait. I barely recognized your mother, she's gained so much weight.

- I'm so excited to see from your recent photo that you're pregnant! I didn't even know you and your hubby were trying.

- Where did you get all these liberal friends? I'm sure they are nice, even though the level of ignorance they display is appalling.

- Did your sister tell you to call me? She has some secret she won't reveal and I think you should fill me in.

- Interesting photo of the burger with the donut buns. Are you sure you should be eating that? Didn't your father die of a heart attack? Just asking.
- I'm sorry to see you are sick. And surprised, since you told me you were taking a mental health day today.
- Did you get that new job? I hope so!
- So sorry to hear your daughter broke up with her boyfriend. I always thought she was too good for him anyway.

Commenting about things that should be confidential, talking about other people, and making insensitive remarks are never appropriate for Facebook or anyplace else. Remember, nothing on the Internet is ever really private or ever really goes away.

There's so much good that can be done through online communication. It does offer many opportunities to share with others, to speak truth, to spread light in the darkness. But the speed of the Internet and our flying fingers on the keyboard can get in the way of finding the perfect words.

Nobody ever said there was a rule against planning what you post, or even writing a rough draft before you type it up and hit Send or Submit. That way you can use your cyberspace powers for good instead of evil, right?

What Others Say: Quotes Worth Sharing

Apathy is the glove into which evil slips its hand.

Bodie Thoene

Too often we enjoy the comfort of opinion without the discomfort of thought.

John F. Kennedy

It is impossible to defeat an ignorant man in argument.

William G. Mcadoo

A half-truth is a whole lie.

Yiddish Proverb

Simple solutions seldom are.

Forbes magazine

The clash of ideas is the sound of freedom.

Graffiti

One has the right to be wrong in a democracy.

Claude Pepper

The most prominent place in hell is reserved for those who are neutral on the great issues of life.

Billy Graham

Be bold in what you stand for and careful what you fall for.

Ruth Boorstin, in the *Wall Street Journal*

Scripture Passages to Read or Quote

My servant Job will pray for you, and I will accept his prayer and not deal with you according to your folly. You have not spoken the truth about me, as my servant Job has.

Job 42:8

Lord, who may dwell in your sacred tent?
Who may live on your holy mountain?
The one whose walk is blameless,
who does what is righteous,
who speaks the truth from their heart;

whose tongue utters no slander,
who does no wrong to a neighbor,
and casts no slur on others.

Psalm 15:1–3

There are those who hate the one who upholds justice in court and detest the one who tells the truth.

Amos 5:10

He has shown you, O mortal, what is good. And what does the Lord require of you? To act justly and to love mercy and to walk humbly with your God.

Micah 6:8

This is what the Lord Almighty said: "Administer true justice; show mercy and compassion to one another."

Zechariah 7:9

Whoever speaks on their own does so to gain personal glory, but he who seeks the glory of the one who sent him is a man of truth; there is nothing false about him.

John 7:18

You belong to your father, the devil, and you want to carry out your father's desires. He was a murderer from the beginning, not holding to the truth, for there is no truth in him. When he lies, he speaks his native language, for he is a liar and the father of lies.

John 8:44

We have different gifts, according to the grace given to each of us. If your gift is prophesying, then prophesy in accordance with your faith; if it is serving, then serve; if it is teaching, then teach; if it is to encourage, then give encouragement; if it is giving, then give generously; if it is to lead, do it diligently; if it is to show mercy, do it cheerfully.

Romans 12:6–8

All of us also lived among them at one time, gratifying the cravings of our flesh and following its desires and thoughts. Like the rest, we were by nature deserving of wrath. But because of his great love for us, God, who is rich in mercy, made us alive with Christ even when we were dead in transgressions—it is by grace you have been saved.

Ephesians 2:3–5

Love does not delight in evil but rejoices with the truth.

1 Corinthians 13:6

I thank Christ Jesus our Lord, who has given me strength, that he considered me trustworthy, appointing me to his service. Even though I was once a blasphemer and a persecutor and a violent man, I was shown mercy because I acted in ignorance and unbelief. The grace of our Lord was poured out on me abundantly, along with the faith and love that are in Christ Jesus.

1 Timothy 1:12–14

And the peace of God, which transcends all understanding, will guard your hearts and your minds in Christ Jesus.

Finally, brothers and sisters, whatever is true, whatever is noble, whatever is right, whatever is pure, whatever is lovely, whatever is admirable—if anything is excellent or praiseworthy—think about such things. Whatever you have learned or received or heard from me, or seen in me—put it into practice. And the God of peace will be with you.

Philippians 4:7–9

But the wisdom that comes from heaven is first of all pure; then peace-loving, considerate, submissive, full of mercy and good fruit, impartial and sincere.

James 3:17

Grace, mercy and peace from God the Father and from Jesus Christ, the Father's Son, will be with us in truth and love.

2 John 1:3

Notes

1. Michael Murray and James Wang, "Secretary of Defense Robert Gates on Why He's Ready to Retire," June 6, 2011, http://abcnews.go.com/US/time-secretary-defense-robert-gates-ready-retire/story?id=13772606#.T0UHX3rvZBk.

2. "Kind-hearted patron honored couple with dinner," *Colorado Springs Gazette,* August 3, 2005, www.gazette.com/opinion/money-12431-voters-people.html.

3. "Ask Amy," Amy Dickinson, *The Denver Post,* June 8, 2011.

4. Adapted from Etiquette Hell, www.etiquettehell.com/content/eh_wedding/invites/einvites2001arc.shtml, accessed February 9, 2012.

5. "Should You Announce Your Engagement on Facebook?" Maura Kelly, *Marie Claire,* June 14, 2010, www.marieclaire.com/sex-love/dating-blog/engagement-announcements-on-facebook-status.

6. "Atheists' Billboard Falsely Attributes Quote to Thomas Jefferson," *Huffington Post,* October 27, 2011, http://www.huffingtonpost.com/2011/12/10/atheists-billboard-thomas-jefferson_n_1035168.html.

Liz Duckworth is the author of critically acclaimed books such as *Wildflower Living* and *Ragtail Remembers*. With almost twenty years of experience in the Christian publishing field, Liz heads up Liz Duckworth Publishing Services. She lives in Colorado Springs, Colorado, with her husband and two sons.

OLA.

773 - 443 - 5570